THE CATHOLIC VIEWPOINT SERIES

Editor: John J. Delaney

Neil G. McCluskey, S.J.

CATHOLIC VIEWPOINT
ON EDUCATION

FOREWORD BY
RT. REV. MONSIGNOR FREDERICK G. HOCHWALT

HANOVER HOUSE
Garden City, New York

Imprimi Potest: Thomas E. Henneberry, S.J.
               Provincial, New York Province
               Society of Jesus

Nihil Obstat: Daniel V. Flynn, J.C.D.
               Censor Librorum

Imprimatur:✠Francis Cardinal Spellman
               Archbishop of New York
               August 5, 1959

The nihil obstat and imprimatur are official declarations
that a book or pamphlet is free of doctrinal or moral error.
No implication is contained therein that those who have
granted the nihil obstat and imprimatur agree with the
contents, opinions, or statements expressed.

LIBRARY OF CONGRESS CATALOG CARD NUMBER 59–13979

Copyright © 1959, by Doubleday & Company, Inc.
Designed by Joseph P. Ascherl
Printed in the United States of America
All Rights Reserved

To my teachers, all of them,
who shared with me their
viewpoints—catholic and Catholic.

Contents

Foreword

Hundreds of volumes and millions of words have been written about public education in the United States to bring about a better public understanding of what public education is and what it is trying to achieve. But the private schools, especially the parochial schools, have not been nearly so fortunate. The productivity of authors writing in these areas has left much to be desired. The supporters of private education have been pleading for a good exposition of their cause and Father Neil McCluskey, S. J., has met the challenge in a most helpful way.

From his vantage point as an editor and an educator, and assisted by his close contacts with the National Catholic Welfare Conference, the National Catholic Educational Association, and the Jesuit Educational Association, the author has set down in eight chapters a well-rounded presentation of a Catholic viewpoint on education. The book does not deal with any of the controversies or problems of college education but, nevertheless, takes in the sweep of America's school history. The development of both private and public education, side by side, is spelled out and it is emphasized that America's schools in the beginning were religious schools. Father McCluskey neatly summarizes the contest between the two forms of education, and high-lights the major decisions taken as a result by the Councils of Baltimore.

The chapter on the Price of Pluralism will perhaps be the most valuable reading for the Catholic layman who for the first time is afforded a chance to master the challenge that the parochial schools present a divisive force in the mainstream of American life. Here Father McCluskey emphasizes that the American people have always honored the principle of respect for cultural diversity and have pursued an ideal course between the extremes of totalitarian uniformity and chaotic individualism. The author is at his best when defining the sharp distinction between "state" and "society."

In dealing with the national policy of excluding religion, at least in the traditional sense, Father McCluskey is returning to a theme he developed in another recently compiled book, *Public Schools and Moral Education*. The layman, as well as the educator, will read with great profit and interest those pages which demonstrate how the secularists' philosophy more and more dominates public education, hidden all too often under the beguiling term of "democratic humanism." It is clearly pointed out that secularist educators have adopted the language of the churches with skillful effect. "It is consoling," says the author, "for families with religious backgrounds to be blandly assured that in promoting social unity the common schools are achieving a genuine religious unity." But the religion meant here, of course, is the secularist faith in humanity itself, as it evolves in American democratic society, and has nothing to do with religion in the time-honored sense.

The sections of the book which may be put to greatest use may be those which deal with the question of financial support for education. The year-by-year increase in the burden which young Catholic taxpayers and parents must carry makes it imperative that the entire nation look harder than ever for a solution to the problem of paying for education, both public and private.

Father McCluskey's book will go a long way toward getting what Catholic parents want right now. They want a sympathetic hearing for their case, public recognition of their problem, and the necessary help to work for an equitable solution. Although general federal aid for parochial schools may be both undesirable and unconstitutional, certain peripheral services can be considered, such as bus transportation, certain reading materials, health services, and other items which are now provided under the National Defense Education Act of 1958. Parents undoubtedly would be interested, too, in the long-term, low-interest-rate loans for schoolhouse construction for private schools.

In the hands of laymen and educators, *Catholic Viewpoint on Education* will do much to clarify the Catholic position for Catho-

lics and non-Catholics alike. Brief though it is, it will become a
ready reference point for the troubled area of education. For my-
self I am deeply grateful to the author and publishers for bringing
together between two covers so many important educational facts
and compelling ideas.

FREDERICK G. HOCHWALT

CATHOLIC VIEWPOINT ON EDUCATION

CHAPTER 1

Prologue and Preliminary

It is sometimes embarrassing to look history in the face. And yet the only way to avoid repeating yesterday's failures and partial successes, as well as to plan wisely for tomorrow's advances, is to have some acquaintance with what already has taken place. A Catholic viewpoint on education, accordingly, takes in the sweep of America's school history.

When the first settlers came to North American shores, they brought with them the ideas, the language, the religion, and the general culture of the countries they left behind. The social institutions they had known in the Old World were the models they strove to re-create on the shores of *New* Spain, or *New* France, or *New* England, or *New* Amsterdam.[1] The schools they built in the early colonial period were generally indistinguishable from schools in Spain, France, England, or Holland. In building them the colonists had in mind the same curriculum, the same purposes, and the same class of people served by the schools in the old country, and yet, when social institutions are transplanted, they tend to take on the coloring of their new environment. The same process

[1] To the Spanish Franciscans goes the distinction of having made the first beginnings of education within the present confines of the United States. In 1606 they opened a classical school in St. Augustine, Fla., but it shared the fate of practically all pioneer missionary activity in the Southeast and Southwest, shortly dying out. During the seventeenth century Indian schools were established in the Mississippi Valley, around the Great Lakes, and in northern Maine by missionaries from Canada. In 1722 the Capuchin Fathers started a boys' school in New Orleans, four years after the founding of the city, and in 1727 the Ursuline Sisters made their foundation there. The great centers of Spanish and French Catholic influence, however, existed mostly outside the present boundaries of the United States.

which slowly transformed the European colonies into the United States of America changed European schools into American institutions with decidedly New World characteristics. The Catholic schools likewise were strongly affected by these influences, so much so that the development of the modern Catholic parochial or private school cannot be fully understood except in the broader current of American culture.

There are three general patterns discernible in tracing the origins of education in the American colonies. These patterns are geographical, reflecting different modes of life in the colonies of New England, the South, and the Middle Atlantic regions. The character of the pioneer schools in all three regions, however, was largely molded by the same social forces: institutionalized religion and class structure.

The characterization of the colonial schools as "children of the church" was nowhere more accurate than in the New England colonies, where the extension of the Old World understanding that schools were a normal means for instilling confessional loyalty had been sharpened in the Puritan mind by persecution in England. The conception of the school as an instrument for maintaining the economic structure of a class society was also a European tradition, and the Massachusetts Body of Liberties and other early legal codes prescribed as firmly for the training of children in useful trades as in knowledge of the catechism. Pauperism, no less than religious laxity, was a threat to the tightly knit Puritan community.

It was in the Commonwealth of Massachusetts that the first general school law in the nation was passed. This has come to be known as the Old Deluder Act of 1647. Since the "Old Deluder," Satan, aimed to keep men from the knowledge of the Scriptures, "as in former times by keeping them in an unknown tongue, so in these times by persuading from the use of tongues," the present Act would thwart him by requiring every township with fifty householders to appoint a teacher and provide a school. Parents of pupils would pay the teacher or he might be paid out of tax funds, if the town meeting so decided. Here was enunciated for the first time among English-speaking peoples the principle that public authority had the right to *require* individual communities to establish and maintain schools.

Historians are divided, however, in their interpretations of what precisely was involved. One standard history[2] says that this law and a similar but less specific law of 1642 are the foundation of the present American public school system, but another dismisses this claim, saying that in no American sense does this appear to be a provision for public schools.[3] This much, however, seems clear: the principle was acted upon that public authority may regulate and promote education as a matter of public concern. In a theocracy, taxes and tithes, parish and civic business, secular and religious affairs easily blend together and lose their identity, so that it is not always easy to see where church authority leaves off and civil authority begins. Nonetheless, the primary purpose of these and similar laws was the preservation and extension of the Congregational faith. Moreover, the legal control of the schools was ecclesiastical rather than secular, and religious instruction was universally considered the school's first responsibility toward the child. The New England communities had a great advantage over other regions in being able to establish common schools. There the colonists not only spoke the same language, had the same customs and hailed from the same country, but, for the most part, were united in their allegiance to the Protestant Congregationalism of John Calvin.[4]

The school pattern that developed in the southern colonies is best exemplified by Virginia. Religious influence was pervasive in the schools of the South also, but not in the same way as in the New England schools. The settlers in the southern colonies had not left the mother country because of religious persecution. The church they brought with them was the established Church of England to which the majority loyally adhered. The Anglican

[2] Ellwood P. Cubberley, *Public Education in the United States,* revised and enlarged ed. (Boston: Houghton Mifflin Co., 1947), p. 18.

[3] Edgar W. Knight, *Education in the United States,* 3rd ed. (Boston: Ginn and Co., 1951), p. 105. The author says that the authority behind these laws was that of the Puritan congregation "which was identical with the state but was more powerful than it."

[4] Down to the time of the Revolution the textbooks used for instruction were the Hornbook, the *Primer,* the Psalter, the Testament, and the Bible. The Hornbook was the child's first book. He learned his letters and began to spell out the words of the Our Father printed on a board which was protected from dirty fingers by a thin sheet of transparent horn. The New England *Primer* was basically a children's version of the Calvinist catechism. Between 1700 and 1850 the *Primer* sold 3 million copies.

clergy had complete control of the schools throughout the seventeenth century, a control which they yielded only by degrees in the following century. An order issued in 1688, requiring all schoolmasters to appear before the General Court in order to present testimonials of their competency and proof "that they were upright and sober in their lives, and conformable in their religious opinions to the doctrines of the Church of England," is indicative of this close ecclesiastical supervision.[5]

The plantation, rather than the town, became the social and economic unit, and this militated against the kind of centralized school system that arose in New England. Differences in educational opportunities were more pronounced than in New England. Here, the professional class—which included the large planters and ordinary landowners—maintained a system of schooling separate from the ordinary schools. The well-to-do children began their education with private tutors or in one of the small endowed schools which were privately conducted. For the less fortunate there were some charity schools under church sponsorship but the state, generally speaking, remained aloof. Whatever "public" schooling existed was intended for orphans and the children of the poor, and it would be long years before this association, amounting almost to a stigma, would be shed by the public school.

The third pattern of school development, and the one to which the few pioneer Catholic schools of the United States belonged, was that of the middle colonies, best typified by Pennsylvania. From the earliest years a variety of nations were represented among the immigrants that flocked to the Quaker colony. The Dutch and Swedes had moved up the Delaware even prior to 1681, when Charles II made his royal land grant to William Penn. The Quakers successfully publicized their colonial venture throughout Holland and Germany as well as in the British Isles. There was no established church in the colony and initially the government proclaimed freedom for all.[6]

Pennsylvania's benevolent attitude ensured almost continual

[5] Commonly the teachers were licensed by the Archbishop of Canterbury or the Bishop of London. In both Virginia and New York the ministers examined teachers salaried by the provincial government, mainly to ensure religious orthodoxy.

[6] From 1708 to 1742 a series of acts was passed which barred Catholics from citizenship and from the purchase of land.

freedom for educational activities by the different religious groups, so that from the early years of the colony there were parochial schools, that is, schools sponsored by church "parishes" in contrast to town or private sponsorship. There were schools under the direction of Moravians, Mennonites, Quakers, Lutherans, Presbyterians, Baptists—and even Catholics. Throughout the colonial period the school pattern in New York and New Jersey approximated that of the Quaker colony.

Of the three regional patterns just described, the one that furnished the model for the American public schools during the nineteenth century was that which emerged from the culturally homogeneous Puritan colonies of New England. From Massachusetts and Connecticut, New Englanders brought their common school and the assumptions underlying it to western New York, upper Pennsylvania and, especially, to Ohio and the western lands out of which the first new states were to be carved. Between the War of the Revolution and the close of the War of 1812, however, education in American schools developed slowly. During these years there was little money or energy to be expended on schools, for the attention of the young nation was directed to the more pressing problems of survival.

The public school, in its essential form, took shape during the next fifty years—the period between the close of the War of 1812 and the outbreak of the Civil War in 1861. The development of such a school was a response to particular conditions in American society. The idea of a "common" public school could hardly have materialized except for two movements of vast consequence that characterized nineteenth-century America: the liberalizing of Protestant Christianity and the release of the dynamisms latent in a popular democracy. A few words should be said about each.

Sectarian differences among the groups who colonized America had set them apart. Differences in belief and church organization, often accentuated by diversity of tongue and nationality, were a source of friction, mistrust, even of hostility. It was true that the settlers of America shared belief in a Supreme Being who had created man for an immortal destiny to be achieved through man's faith and/or good works. Even the small number of early Americans who did not call themselves Christians agreed on a theistically based natural law as the ultimate motive of right conduct. The overwhelming majority, however, also accepted the basic ideas of the Christian revelation and gave allegiance to some form of Christian orthodoxy, ordinarily in an institutionalized form, which centered about the person and mission of Jesus Christ, the Saviour revealed in the Bible.

The stiffness built on differences of belief and ritual underwent a gradual loosening, and by the eve of the Revolution "liberal" religious or even purely secular attitudes toward human problems were increasingly common. Among the chief influences that led to the blunting of theological differences and the parallel process of secularization of American life during the nineteenth century were the liberal philosophies of the preceding century, usually referred to as the Age of the Enlightenment. The rationalism, empiricism, and skepticism of the period challenged the worth of tradition and the need for authority in social, political, and religious thought. In England, France, and several other continental countries, there was a small but influential class, who, though still regarding themselves as Christians, rejected revealed religion and accepted the Bible only as a natural literary expression of ethical truths. The wounding of human nature through Adam's original sin and the need for redemption were specific doctrines discarded in favor of the conviction that human nature was infinitely perfectible and that man need only apply his reason to improve his condition on every level. This became the *point de départ* of British and American Unitarianism.

The more liberal Christianity of the early nineteenth century prepared the soil for the common school idea. It softened differences in belief and ritual among the different Protestant religious groups, enabling them to co-operate in a common educational enterprise, and it stressed the role of education in improving the temporal lot of the individual and of society. The new religious outlook, by transcending the individual Protestant sect, made possible a "nonsectarianism," which could remain Protestant and yet not belong to a particular Protestant sect.

The second movement which helped bring the public school into being was the growing realization of what democracy meant in practice. The educated aristocracy that had led the colonial struggle to a successful conclusion and had written its political philosophy into a Constitution and Bill of Rights was a minority. In fact, the number of those eligible for the franchise in our first national balloting was very small. In the election of 1789 which put George Washington into office as first President, approximately one free male in seven was able to vote, since all thirteen states had some form of property or poll-tax qualification for suffrage. These conditions, however, were shortly to be swept away in the exuberance of popular democracy, whose high-water mark was reached in the presidential victory of Andrew Jackson in 1828.

There were many leaders in the first years of the American Republic who saw that the distinctive character of the republican form of government required an informed and literate citizenry as its base. The monarchical and class forms of government in Europe had been rejected, but full participation in a republic presupposed an educated citizenry, and this meant in turn that schooling had to be available for all. Among these farsighted men was Horace Mann, honored today as the "Father of the Public School."

In the 1830s Mann, who was the first to hold the post of secretary of the Massachusetts State Board of Education, emerged as the most important educational figure in the nation. There were of course prominent men elsewhere—mainly New Englanders—who played leading roles in the public school movement. Among them were Henry Barnard, who occupied a position similar to Mann's in Connecticut and Rhode Island; Samuel Lewis and Calvin E. Stowe in Ohio; Caleb Mills in Indiana; and Calvin H. Wiley in North Carolina. Yet Mann and Massachusetts most influenced the development of public school education.

Mann came on the scene when the feeling was growing that education was not merely something to be encouraged by the civil authority but a function to be directly undertaken. This attitude was dictated by a number of reasons, none more compelling than the growing awareness that the church-sponsored and private schools were not providing for all children. Frequently it did happen that the children of the better classes were the only ones for whom adequate provision was made in religious schools. Even during the early decades of the nineteenth century, the school was still looked upon pretty much as a private undertaking, ordinarily the business of the church or of private initiative with some sort of ecclesiastical or clerical supervision. When the drive for universal education got under way, however, the evangelical sects —Methodist and Baptist mainly—were overtaking in numbers and influence the older Protestant churches. The newer groups had no tradition of church-controlled schools and had little difficulty in accepting government control of education. Even without the complication resulting from the waves of immigrants, private and church resources would have been hard put to cope with the demand for schools.

Puritan Congregationalism had been the cement binding the Commonwealth together, but even before Mann began to organize public schooling, differences over articles of dogmatic belief between orthodox and liberal Congregationalists had shattered the old unity. The liberals broke with established Congregationalism and came to be known as Unitarians. In 1825 the American Unitarian Association was formed, and eight years later the Congregational Church lost its favored position in Massachusetts law.

The new legal equality of all churches did not mean, however, that the traditional religious emphasis on education had been interrupted. On the contrary, the desire for a religious orientation and for a religiously based moral training within the common public school was still universal. There was, in fact, a Commonwealth law, dating from 1789 and re-enacted in 1826, which charged all those engaged in education to form character in Massachusetts children through suitable instruction in "piety." The problem, though, was how this could be done in the schools without favoring the set of beliefs and practices of one particular church.

Horace Mann left no doubt in anyone's mind of his attitude toward the clerically dominated sectarian education that had long endured in Massachusetts: it was a miserable failure, from which he argued that the only agency left for properly inculcating moral training was that of the "nonsectarian" public school. Nonetheless, he very much wanted Christianity—according to his own understanding of it—to be in the public schools. Our great duty as educators, as friends and sustainers of the common school system, he said, is to train the children up in "the love of God and the love of man; to make the perfect example of Jesus Christ lovely in their eyes." This duty entailed the giving to all children "so much religious instruction as is compatible with the rights of others and with the genius of our government." Mann would leave to parents and guardians all special and peculiar instruction respecting politics and theology, and "at last, when the children arrive at years of maturity, to commend them to that inviolable prerogative of private judgment and of self-direction, which in a Protestant and a Republican country, is the acknowledged birthright of every human being."[7] Mann argued that there was a common core of Christian religious beliefs which could be taught in the common school without objection, leaving the elaboration of this frame to the home and church. Despite the diversity of doctrines in the community, there were many points of agreement, and these would constitute "the best possible preparation for each to proceed in adding those distinctive particulars, deemed necessary to a complete and perfect faith." Religion was to remain in the public schools, but it was to be no longer identifiable as Congregational or Methodist or Episcopal. It was simply to be "nonsectarian."

Horace Mann's personal idea of Christianity was basically Locke's Christian deism with a thick overlay of phrenology.[8] Christianity for Mann was the Christianity of the Ten Commandments, the Golden Rule, the Beatitudes, the example of Christ and other biblical characters—in sum, the moral and ethical aspects of the religion revealed in the Bible. He explained that his system "founds its morals on the basis of religion; it welcomes the religion of the Bible"; and in receiving the Bible, "it allows it to do what it is allowed to do in no other system—*to speak for itself.*" Mann appealed to the classical Protestant principle that "the Bible is the acknowledged expositor of Christianity," and "in strictness, Christianity has no other authoritative expounder." He wanted the Bible to go into the public schools "enshielded from harm, by the great Protestant doctrine of the inviolability of conscience,

[7] There is a complete discussion of this issue in Neil G. McCluskey, *Public Schools and Moral Education* (New York: Columbia Univ. Press, 1958), pp. 32–98.

[8] Phrenology was a primitive behavioristic psychology united to a theory of localized brain functions. Phrenologists believed that moral and intellectual traits could be discovered by studying the shape of the head in conjunction with some knowledge of temperament.

the right and sanctity of private judgment, without note or interpreter."

Yet Mann was continually under the necessity of absolving himself from charges that he was an enemy of religious instruction in the schools. His defense was that he meant only to exclude specific *sectarian* doctrines, or "man-made" creeds, and to these he was opposing universally accepted Christianity—what he called the "religion of heaven." His opponents retorted that in his zeal to keep sectarian religious teaching out of the common schools, he had espoused a number of theological positions which smacked strongly of rationalism or Lockian deism, and certainly were the substance of Unitarianism.

In addition to what can be fairly viewed as Mann's private missionary motives, there was a practical side to all this. In promoting his "nonsectarian," biblically based, liberal Protestant Christianity, Horace Mann was likewise effecting a workable compromise to protect the equal position of the different Protestant churches and sects in the common schools. Despite the reservations of some Protestant groups regarding this position and its assumption of Christian unity around the Bible, Mann's principle was almost universally adopted. It worked and, therefore, it became basic to the public school philosophy of character education. Granted the conditions of those times, almost any other approach but Mann's compromise would have meant the disintegration of the common school movement. Horace Mann kept the great symbol of Protestantism, the Bible, in the schools but would not permit any sectarian interpretation of it. A general Protestant Christian influence should permeate the schools, but all specific sectarian influence was to be shut out.

If the Mann solution was only grudgingly accepted by a considerable part of the Protestant community, what of the Catholics? Catholics found themselves faced with a serious problem of conscience, and as their numbers increased their problem became more and more a national one.

During the century and a half of the colonial period, the Roman Catholic Church in America can be said to have lived in the catacombs. Catholics were suspected and feared. As a group, they lived their lives outside the cultural and political activities of the community. Though many of the more onerous disabilities and penalties were lifted at the opening of the national period, only four states in their constitutional conventions gave Catholics political equality with Protestants.

The rigid penal legislation in existence in every colony at the time of the Revolution—modeled on that of the mother country—curtailed the freedom of Catholics to worship, to participate in civic life, and to educate their children. The school situation was particularly intolerable. The schools were belligerently Protestant. The hymns, homilies, and prayers in common use contained references derogatory to the Catholic Church. The texts and books were filled with crude distortions of history and dogma calculated to perpetuate hatred of "Popery."[9] The Catholic child was made to feel out of place in the colonial school, and yet his parents were liable to a stiff fine if they sent him out of the colonies for his education. Catholics themselves were barred from teaching. Even in Catholic-founded Maryland the legislature in 1704 had passed "An Act to Prevent the Growth of Popery," among whose bristling provisions was one that threatened any Catholic with deportation, who should keep school, board students, or instruct children.

Earlier, however, the first Catholic school in the British colonies had been established in Maryland by the Jesuits. Records are dim and incomplete, but the foundation seems to have been made about 1640 at Saint Mary's City. Under normal conditions this school might well have been what it never had the chance to be:

[9] The New England *Primer* contained a celebrated caricature of the Pope. The artist depicted a towering ugly figure whose head was crowned with a tiara. Lines designated by letters radiated from different parts of the body. On the opposite page the children could find the explanation of the diagram:

Advise to Children

Child, behold that Man of Sin, the *Pope*, worthy of thy utmost hatred.

Thou shall find in his Head, (A) *Heresy*.

In his Shoulders, (B) *the Supporters of Disorder*.

In his Heart, (C) *Malice, Murder and Treachery*.

In his Arms, (D) *Cruelty*.

In his Knees, (E) *False Worship and Idolatry*.

In his Feet, (F) *Swiftness to shed Blood*.

In his Stomach, (G) *Insatiable Covetousness*.

In his Lyons, (H) *the worst of Lusts*.

a collegiate institution whose venerability would today equal Harvard's.[10]

The next recorded foundation was probably in 1673 at Newton, a center of underground Catholic activity in the Maryland colony. The Revolution of 1688 which chased James II from his throne and put his Protestant daughter Mary and her husband William of Orange thereon further darkened Catholic fortunes on the other side of the Atlantic. The Newton School was closed, as was another brief-lived Jesuit school in New York City.[11] The next attempt, the school at Bohemia Manor in the northeast corner of Maryland, seems to have been favored by its proximity to more tolerant Pennsylvania, for it was in operation from 1744 until it had to close in 1765. During these few years the scions of many old Catholic families were enrolled at Bohemia Manor, including the Neales, Brents, and Carrolls. Some fifteen other Catholic schools, many of them for the children of German immigrants, were begun in Pennsylvania prior to the Revolution.

Catholic and Protestant colonists made common cause during the War of the Revolution. The leadership of prominent men like Charles Carroll, Thomas FitzSimmons, and Daniel Carroll; the proved loyalty of the immigrant Irish, German, and French Catholics; the vigorous support of the old Maryland families; the popular alliance with Catholic France—all these factors brought increased respect for the little Catholic community, whose estimated numbers at the start of the national period were 30,000. Even more important than these factors in explaining the rapid growth of the Catholic Church was the triumph of the political philosophy that acknowledged the equal status in federal law of

[10] That an institution of higher than elementary level was projected by the Maryland Jesuits can be gathered from a letter written to them by Father Mutius Vitelleschi, General of the Society, dated September 16, 1640: "The hope held out of a college I am happy to entertain; and when it shall have matured, I will not be backward in extending my approval." (See Thomas Hughes, *History of the Society of Jesus in North America, Colonial and Federal. Documents* I, No. 5. R.)

[11] About 1684 the Episcopal Church began an institution for boys on the site of New York City's Old Trinity Church, at Broadway and Wall Street, which shortly closed its doors. One of the Jesuits who landed in the town in 1684 reopened the school at the request of the Catholic governor, Thomas Dongan.

all church groups, and the freedom of every individual to practice his religion unmolested.

The second war of independence, fought between 1812 and 1815 with Britain, proved to the world that the United States of America was going to survive as a nation. Though emigrants by the thousands had streamed to American shores during the last decades of the eighteenth century, the flow now rose to tidal proportions. The political turbulence on the Continent sent many Catholics from France and Germany; the ruin of the woolen industry and the famines of the 1840s brought boatloads of Irish Catholics. By 1820 the Catholic population was reckoned at 195,000; a decade later, it was 318,000; in 1840, 663,000; in 1850, 1,606,000. The total doubled again before 1860, and doubled again in both the census of 1880 and 1900.[12]

Until 1815 the numerically insignificant group of Catholics had not been a cause of general concern for the young Protestant nation. But this situation soon changed. Protestant-Catholic amity was short-lived, and the status of Catholics in the land of religious liberty became anomalous indeed.

The anti-Catholicism that marked the decades before the Civil War, however, was seldom found in an undiluted form. The hundreds of thousands of Irish and German Catholics who entered the United States during these years were, to begin with, foreigners. Between 1830 and 1840 the immigrants amounted to only about 3 per cent of the total population but in the next ten years made up nearly 7 per cent. Such an influx by itself would have upset a small populace long isolated from direct European influence. The Irish, however, brought with them their strong love for the Church of St. Patrick and their enthusiastic hatred of the English. The German immigrants, for their part, tending to identify the German language and culture with their Catholicism, sturdily defended both against the encroachments of New World civilization. The immigrants were disdained, resented, and feared by native Americans. Their Old World customs and language made them annoyingly different. Their cheap labor flooding the market represented an economic threat. Above everything, however, as com-

[12] See John L. Thomas, *The American Catholic Family* (Englewood Cliffs, N.J.: Prentice-Hall, Inc., 1956), p. 108. *The Official Catholic Directory for 1959* gives the American Catholic population as 39,505,475.

municants of the Roman Church they were, in their growing numbers, suspected of endangering the dearly won liberties of Protestant America. The Catholic immigrant was feared, consequently, for more than his Catholicism.

Franklin K. Lane, President Wilson's Secretary of the Interior, once offered this tongue-in-the-cheek description of the Americanization process: "One part ability to read, write and speak English; one part the Declaration of Independence; one part the Constitution; one part love for apple pie; one part desire and willingness to wear American shoes; and another part pride in American plumbing will make an American of anyone."[13]

Through the nineteenth century the Protestant Bible could also have been included in the recipe. For very many citizens the Bible was only slightly less a patriotic symbol than the American flag, and in their eyes Bible and flag together were the alchemy which transformed Europeans into true Americans. Nativism looked to Protestant Christianity as the source and guarantee of its moral influence. The popular conception of how to Americanize immigrants, therefore, had to involve in some way teaching the newly arrived the moral and spiritual beliefs which undergirded American republicanism. This was the justification for missionary work on the part of zealous nativists. Their campaign to "Christianize" the immigrants was, in the case of Catholic newcomers, thinly disguised Protestant proselytizing. The dozens of religious journals of the period titillated their readers regularly with accounts of the conversion of Irish servant girls from the ecclesiastical tyranny of the Old World or of how the discovery of the Bible had opened the eyes of some German laborer to the meaning of American freedom.

Compulsory reading of the Bible was a major Catholic grievance in the unending school controversies of those decades of adjustment. In New York in 1840 a spokesman for Archbishop John Hughes put the point frankly:

> The Holy Scriptures are read every day, with the restriction that no specific tenets are to be inculcated. Here we find the great demarcating principle between the Catholic Church and

---

[13] Quoted by William C. Smith, *Americans in the Making* (New York: Appleton-Century-Crofts, 1939), p. 116.

the Sectaries introduced silently. The Catholic Church tells her children they must be taught by *authority*. The Sectaries say, read the Bible, judge for yourselves. The Protestant principle is therefore acted upon, slyly inculcated, and the schools are Sectarian.[14]

That there was serious leakage from the Church is a matter beyond dispute. Bishop Bernard J. McQuaid of Rochester, N.Y. could quote a famous Presbyterian minister as openly avowing "that the Bible and the Common Schools were two stones of the mill that would grind Catholicity out of Catholics," and a Methodist minister as boasting that in twelve years the Catholics had lost 1,900,000 children.[15]

Catholic efforts to obtain relief from this intolerable situation took two forms. The bishops asked that Catholic youngsters in the public schools be excused from classroom reading and discussion of the Protestant Bible, and that the school taxes collected from Catholic parents be used to educate their children in church schools. As one member of the hierarchy stated the Catholic position: "It is not to deprive Protestants of their Bible in their schools; it is to educate Catholic children in Catholic schools with our own money, under state supervision if you please. We do not want Protestant money, nor any state money that was not taken from our purses."[16]

In the matter of Bible reading the courts offered no redress for Catholic petitioners. In fact, strong legal support for the religious *status quo* in the public schools was supplied by an 1854 ruling of the Maine Supreme Court (*Donahue* v. *Richards*), allowing school authorities to compel the reading of the King James version of the Bible. This precedent held for nearly forty years. In Boston and New York Catholic students were expelled from the public schools for refusing to read the Protestant Bible. Only in 1890 did a Wisconsin court in the much agitated Edgerton Bible case reverse the precedent set in *Donahue* v. *Richards*.

[14] The New York *Freeman's Journal*, July 11, 1840, cited in Edward M. Connors, *Church-State Relationships* (Washington: Catholic Univ. Press, 1951), p. 56.
[15] Quoted in Richard J. Gabel, *Public Funds for Church and Private Schools* (Washington: Catholic Univ. Press, 1937), p. 487.
[16] McQuaid quoted by Gabel, ibid., p. 487.

New York City was the scene of the first important struggle by Catholics to obtain a proportionate share in the common school fund, and the outcome here set a national policy that, with minor exceptions, has endured to the present day.

Between 1795 and 1825 the state had given financial aid to all educational institutions in New York City, most of which were under church auspices. The Free School Society was founded in 1805 "for the education of such poor children as do not belong to, or are not provided for by any religious society." Shortly, it adopted a new title, the Public School Society, and soon became the most powerful educational organization in the city. In 1824 the state legislature authorized the city council to select the institutions for which the state would provide funds. The following year a committee of the council recommended that in the future no distribution of any part of public funds should go to religious societies. Since the school fund, in the opinion of the committee, was "purely of a civil character," it could not be entrusted to religious bodies without "a violation of an elementary principle in the politics of State and country." From 1825 on, New York City's share of the state school fund went exclusively to the nonsectarian Public School Society, except for minor grants to orphanages and mission schools. This, it is interesting to note, was the first major move toward the secularization of the common schools.

The question of state support for religious schools was reopened in 1840, when Governor William H. Seward in his message to the state legislature recommended the establishment of state-supported denominational and language schools for immigrant children. Bishop (later Archbishop) John Hughes publicly urged the justice of the claims of the religious school. In his petition to the council of New York City, he stressed that the basis of the claim by Catholic schools for support was not the religious character of the corporation but their civic character. In other words, he urged that just as Catholic citizens are taxed for the school fund in their capacity as citizens and not as Catholics, so they should be aided as citizens and not as Catholics. The bishop's presentation fell on deaf ears.

Non-Catholics were easily persuaded that the Catholic campaigns to get a share of the common school funds for their own schools and to eliminate the Protestant Bible from the public schools were a concerted attack on the foundations of the Republic. The bitterness engendered over the school question in New York spread to other parts of the nation and fueled the nativist attacks on Catholics that marred the 1840s.[17] In view of the foregoing, it is entirely understandable that the attitude of the Catholic bishops and people hardened to the point where strong measures were taken to protect the religious faith of Catholic children.

The school question and other long accumulated problems of church organization and discipline brought the Catholic bishops of the United States together in 1829 for the first of the seven Provincial Councils of Baltimore that took place between that year and 1849.

In the 1829 meeting the seven bishops prepared a joint letter to American Catholics urging the necessity of Catholic schools. The bishops insisted that the grave danger of loss of faith for Catholic boys and girls, particularly those from poor families, required the establishment of schools free from the defects which, in Catholic eyes, seriously marred available schools. The textbooks were a particularly sore point. "The schoolboy can scarcely find a book," said the bishops, "in which some one or more of our institutions or practices is not exhibited for otherwise than it really is, and greatly to our disadvantage."[18]

By 1840, the year of the fourth council, the situation had shown no improvement. The bishops urged pastors to protest what was still a universal practice: Catholic pupils in the public schools were required to join in reading the Protestant Bible, in reciting Protestant prayers, and in singing Protestant hymns. The anti-Catholic bias in the textbooks was again deplored. The bishops called attention to the fact that their protestations were not prompted through "any unkind feeling" to their fellow citizens, nor through any reluctance to work for the common good of the nation, "but because we have found by a painful experience, that in any common effort it was always expected that our distinctive

---

[17] The most competent treatment of these years is still Ray A. Billington, *The Protestant Crusade*, 1800–1860 (New York: Macmillan, 1938).

[18] Quoted in Peter Guilday, *The National Pastorals of the American Hierarchy* (*1792–1919*) (Washington: N.C.W.C., 1923), p. 28.

principles of religious belief and practice should be yielded to the demands of those who thought proper to charge us with error."[19]

Anxiety hung even heavier over the fifth Provincial Council, convened in 1843. The long-smoldering political nativism had leaped into flames and the cry of "No Popery!" was heard up and down the land. "We have seen with serious alarm," the sixteen bishops said, "efforts made to poison the foundations of public education, by giving it a sectarian hue, and accustoming children to the use of a version of the Bible made under sectarian bias, and placing in their hands books of various kinds replete with offensive and dangerous matter."[20]

In addition to these public exhortations of the entire hierarchy, individual bishops and bishops in regional councils drew up statutes ordering pastors to establish parochial schools and parents to send their children to these institutions. Nowhere was this done with more exactness than in the Midwest. The Second Provincial Council of Cincinnati ordered that all pastors of souls, "under pain of mortal sin," were "to provide a Catholic school in every parish or congregation subject to them, where this can be done." The bishops of this region were largely responsible for the vigor of the decrees on education passed in the fall of 1884 by the Third Plenary Council of Baltimore. One fourth of all the legislation of this last and greatest of the American Church Councils dealt with the school question firmly and in detail. The note of exhortation is absent from the council's words on education; this council decreed.

The seventy-one bishops and archbishops of the council ordered that within two years a parochial school was to be erected near each church and was to be maintained "in perpetuum." Postponement could be allowed only on account of grave difficulties and with episcopal approval. Catholic parents were ordered to send their children to the parochial schools "unless either at home or in other Catholic schools they may sufficiently and evidently provide for the Christian education of their children, or unless it be lawful to send them to other schools on account of a sufficient cause, approved by the bishop, and with opportune cautions and

19 Ibid., p. 134.
20 Ibid., p. 152.

remedies."[21] Where no Catholic school existed or where the existing one was not "fit to educate properly the children in keeping with their station in life," Catholic parents could in good conscience be excused from this obligation. This step, however, required the approval of the local bishop and was to be accompanied by proper provision for the moral and spiritual welfare of the child.

And yet local communities, nonetheless, have periodically attempted to come to terms with the school issue. One of the earliest attempts at compromise occurred in Lowell, Mass., where an arrangement existed between 1831 and 1852 which seemingly had won the approval of the secretary of the State Board of Education, Horace Mann. In a letter to a friend, Mann spoke of the "very intelligent committee," consisting of clergymen and laymen, that entered into an arrangement with the Catholic priests and parents, "by which it was agreed that the teachers of their children should be Catholics." These schools and faculties were subject to the same examination and visitation by the district school committee as other schools and faculties. He referred his correspondent to a number of the *New Englander* "for a minute and interesting account of the whole proceeding."

Similar attempts to combine public and parochial schooling within a single institution were tried widely. Compromise plans existed before the Civil War in the communities of at least ten states: Connecticut, Illinois, Indiana, Kentucky, Michigan, Mississippi, New Jersey, New York, Ohio, and Pennsylvania.[22] In fact, at one time or another in our national history nearly every state in the Union has had some such plan in operation.[23] Children in Catholic schools, of course, were not the only beneficiaries. Identical arrangements were entered into for the benefit of children in Lutheran, Quaker, Presbyterian, Mormon, and other Protestant schools.

The most notable attempts in the last century at these compromises took place at Poughkeepsie, N.Y., and at Faribault,

[21] *Acta et Decreta Concilii Plenarii Baltimorensis III*, Decretum 199 (Baltimore: John Murphy, 1886).

[22] Gabel, pp. 305–6.

[23] Ibid., p. 493.

Minn. The essential features of these plans are identical: (1) An existing parochial school in a heavily populated Catholic locality is leased to the public school district; (2) the district school board operates a "public" school in the parish building, paying maintenance and salary costs; (3) religious instruction and all sectarian exercises are scheduled before or after regular school hours; (4) the school board, with the approval of the pastor, appoints teachers and furnishes textbooks; (5) the school board has full control over examinations, promotions, and general school policies.

Isolated instances of the Poughkeepsie or Faribault "plan" can still be found in some states. These strictly local arrangements have this to be said in their favor: they are inaugurated in good faith and with overwhelming local approval. Yet for several reasons these makeshift arrangements are doomed to fail. A single dissenting voice will invariably rise to challenge the arrangement. Ensuing litigation divides the community and shatters harmony. Prevailing court opinion makes short shrift of such plans, and the community ends up worse off than before. More serious are the national consequences, for any case of this nature becomes magnified into a major church-state issue with resultant socioreligious tensions. Even were the present climate of American public opinion receptive to Poughkeepsie or Faribault plans—which it decidedly is not—Catholics would do well to remember that all such plans fall far short of the ideal Catholic education.

CHAPTER 2

The Price of Pluralism

The problem of religion in education has always been one of the main sources of church-state tensions in the United States. In a letter written in 1890, Cardinal Gibbons explained to Pope Leo XIII that the divisions between Catholics and their fellow citizens "are caused above all by the opposition against the system of national education which is attributed to us, and which, more than any other thing, creates and maintains in the minds of the American people the conviction that the Catholic Church is opposed by principle to the institutions of the country and that a sincere Catholic cannot be a loyal citizen of the United States."[1]

At the beginning of the century there were 854,523 students enrolled in the Catholic primary and secondary schools in the United States. This represented 5.2 per cent of the entire elementary and secondary school population of the nation. In 1958–59 the number had grown to 4.9 million or about 14 per cent of the total enrollment. If the present trend continues, by 1965 Catholic schools will in all probability enroll 6,500,000 students.[2]

A number of educators view this steady expansion with misgivings and have warned that the common public school system as we know it, with its indispensable contribution to unity and

[1] Quoted in John Tracy Ellis, *The Life of James Cardinal Gibbons* (Milwaukee: Bruce, 1952), I, 664.

[2] The 1958–59 figures are taken from *The Official Catholic Directory for 1959*. The estimated total for 1965 is the author's own which is slightly higher than that predicted by the February 1957 estimate of the Office of Education. Since the close of World War II the proportion of the total school population in private and religious schools has shown its sharpest increase, doubling and trebling in many communities. It would have grown still more had the desire of parents been the sole factor to be considered.

common loyalties, may disappear from the American scene. Some of these men have questioned the wisdom of separate schools, and in thoughtful, restrained terms they have called for discussion of the issue. Other voices have been raised which have expressed the same concern in much shriller tones. Despite the nicety or crudity of phrasing, despite the use of circumlocution or epithet, the points made invariably come down to a single charge: divisiveness. The steady expansion of parochial school education disturbs many non-Catholics, because they feel separate schools divide Catholics from other members of the community and do not properly prepare Catholic children for American life.

The case for the public school as social catalyst has been stated by Prof. John W. Dykstra. We quote:

> Now no more effective arrangement for combating religious bigotry could be conceived of than the public school system, which brings together youngsters of every religious faith. In this setting friendship can develop among those of congenial interests and personalities without regard to religious affiliation. Roman Catholic, Protestant and Jewish children play on the same teams, work together in the same clubs, and give allegiance to a common institution. Under these circumstances unflattering generalizations about members of another faith are not readily nurtured.
>
> At the religiously homogeneous school, however, there is no constant assurance that not all Protestants (or Jews or Roman Catholics) have horns. And since the schools increasingly monopolize the students' waking hours with extracurricular programs there is little opportunity for out-of-school contacts with children of other faiths. Moreover, in the religiously segregated schools courses in religion and social studies are likely to be taught from a partisan point of view.[3]

The charge of divisiveness laid at the doors of the parochial schools is a serious one and must be fairly faced by proponents of a separate system of schools for Catholic children. Catholics, for the most part, find it impossible to conceive of themselves as a threat. They are generally unconscious of the anxiety which at times they occasion in their Protestant and non-Catholic neigh-

[3] "Parochial Divisions in American Life," *Christian Century*, April 16, 1958.

bors by the display of their organized strength. Many outsiders, looking at the Catholic Church, see nothing but the closed ranks of a great power structure. And when in the social order they brush against the strong cohesiveness of the Church's collective conscience, they recoil at what seems to them a threat to their civic and religious rights. Since they rightly see in the schools the source of this strength, they raise the issue of parochial school education.

Is there danger in "segregating" school children according to religion? Is the "virus" of separate religious schools "the most debilitating and destructive factor in the American way of life," and is "the present accelerated program of parochial schools" something "not in the American tradition" but "an Old World import"?[4] Are there grounds for the charge that parochial education cannot "meet the requirements of a democracy that rests upon a community of shared educational experience"?[5] Is it truly "unwise for a separate school system to be established," as another critic put it, "because that would lead to divisiveness in the community and mutual bigotry"?[6] How valid is the charge of a former president of Harvard University, who said, "The greater the proportion of our youth who attend independent schools, the greater the threat to our democratic unity"?[7]

No one can deny that unity is fundamental to the well-being of a community. In spite of differences that may originate in conflicting cultural and social backgrounds, the citizens in any society must share some basic values and ideals. They must at least be united in their agreement to live at peace with one another and to work side by side for the essential temporal goals of the community to which they belong. They must give allegiance to the framework of law and legal sanctions which protects the exercise

[4] Maurice J. Thomas, "Voluntary Religious Isolation—Another School Segregation Story," *Phi Delta Kappan*, June 1959.

[5] William Clayton Bower, *Church and State in Education* (Chicago: Univ. of Chicago Press, 1944), pp. 25–26.

[6] William J. Sanders, "Spiritual Values and Public and Religious Education," in *The Public Schools and Spiritual Values*, ed. John S. Brubaker (New York: Harper & Brothers, 1944), p. 101.

[7] James B. Conant, speech to American Association of School Administrators, April 7, 1952.

of individual rights, resolves conflicts of rights, and oversees the discharge of obligations. Quite clearly, without the cement of a shared "public philosophy," as some have entitled it, no society can long maintain the required degree of cohesion. This is all the more true in a representative democracy like our own whose base is common consent and not coercion.

Americans have long looked to the schools to communicate the public philosophy. Historically the common school has been one of the most effective forces in building a sense of the American community. The "melting pot" metaphor is a fitting symbol of the important function performed by the public schools during the periods of the great immigrations. These schools brought immigrant children and the children of immigrants together and imbued them with a common love for their country, the while teaching them respect for their different backgrounds. But here we are at once confronted with the question of balance. Respect for cultural and racial diversity within our national unity is an equally vital part of the Americanizing process whereby we are made *e pluribus unum,* happily phrased in John Courtney Murray's rendition, "one society subsisting amid multiple pluralisms."

Here is the nub of the problem. To what degree can these pluralisms—the distinctive group patterns of behavior arising from ethnic, economic, religious, cultural backgrounds—be encouraged before they weaken the bonds of national unity? How much unity can be required without sacrificing the richness of diversity? What is the norm for deciding when cultural differences disrupt cultural unity, or when these differences are the normal and proper accompaniment of cultural freedom?

American Jewish leaders are continually urging a reorganization of Jewish life in this country in order to preserve "Jewish peoplehood." The president of the American Jewish Congress has reminded American citizens of Jewish origin and religion that they have not only the right but the responsibility to maintain a unity through which they may share in solving common problems and promote common causes.[8] Is it wrong for the Jews in

[8] See New York *Times,* November 22, 1958. In a sermon preached on the occasion of his 40th year in the rabbinate, New York's Dr. Israel Goldstein warned his coreligionists that the great peril to the Jewish future is "the euthanasia of assimilation."

the United States to resist the loss of their group identity in the "mainstream" of American life? For their part, Catholics regard their schools as necessary channels for transmitting the cultural values of Catholicism. Should Catholics abandon separate schools and submerge their cultural identity in some kind of "Mainstream: U.S.A."?

America has never asked this as a condition for citizenship: she is proud to be "one society subsisting amid multiple pluralisms." The government planned by the Founding Fathers was designed to protect differences and to allow minorities to foster their own traditions. Differences of opinion and background were valued as a source of richness and strength for civic life.

Thomas Jefferson argued: "Subject opinion to coercion, and whom will you make your inquisitors? Fallible men; men governed by bad passions, by private as well as public reasons." And to his own question, "Why subject to coercion?" he gave the answer: "To produce uniformity. But is uniformity of opinion desirable? No more than of face and stature." Jefferson singled out difference of opinion in religious matters as something particularly advantageous, for through it "the several sects perform the office of a *censor morum* over each other."[9]

James Madison described the Federal Republic of the United States as a society which "itself will be broken into so many parts, interests, and classes of citizens, that the rights of individuals, or of the minority, will be in little danger from interested combinations of the majority." He insisted that in a free government the security for civil rights must be the same as that for religious rights: "It consists in the one case in the multiplicity of interests, and in the other in the multiplicity of sects."[10]

The American people have always honored the principle of respect for cultural diversity. Except for a few departures, occasioned by brief national hysteria, they have pursued a steady course between the extremes of totalitarian uniformity and chaotic individualism. There is, nonetheless, a tendency inherent in civil authority to strive for a "managed culture," and this temptation is never so beguiling as when the state looks at the malleable minds of its young citizens in school. A single uniform system of

[9] *Notes on Virginia*, Query 17.
[10] *The Federalist*, No. 51.

schooling would be for many of the state's purposes more efficient, manageable, and controllable.

However, the wall of separation between church and state separates two ways. It keeps the church out of state affairs, but it is also supposed to prevent intrusions by civil authority upon ecclesiastical and spiritual domains which are of the cultural order. Dean John C. Bennett of New York's Union Theological Seminary, among others, has warned that "the state in moving so heavily into the field of education has itself crossed any line that might be thought to separate the sphere of the state from the sphere of the Church." Church and state both have a proper interest in the formation of the minds and characters of children but, in the strong language of the U. S. Supreme Court, "the child is not the mere creature of the state" and "those who nurture him and direct his destiny have the right coupled with the high duty, to recognize and prepare him for additional duties." Catholic parents are not satisfied that the present system of state-supported public schools can adequately prepare their children for additional duties and obligations that transcend the realm of Caesar, and so have built their own schools.

The accusation of divisiveness made against the Catholic schools often comes from those schooled in a philosophy which seemingly lays small store by the distinction between "state" and "society"—two terms which are not interchangeable. The state is the people of a society organized for political purposes, and the organ of the state is government. Society, on the other hand, is a much broader concept. Society embraces the sum total of all social organizations, or of men organized to accomplish co-operatively any social goals. In other words, society is much more inclusive than the state. Wherever "state" and "society" are coextensive, the political order becomes identified with the social and cultural aspects of society. This is the meaning of totalitarianism. The more the political power dominates society, the more *total*itarian the state. When the state arbitrarily lays down an official line to be followed in religion or biology or creative writing or education, it has already taken freedom of choice from its citizens. It is axiomatic that in a free society there will be differences of opinion, and that the democratic expression of differences will generate enlightened public policy.

It is fair argument to point out that the alternative to the American pluralistic educational system is the kind of monopolistic system which was imposed upon Germany by the Nazis and flourishes today in Communist Russia and China. Those who scoff at this objection and argue in turn that American education could never become regimented and totalitarian because our schools are controlled locally and not by the federal government miss the argument. There are accidental differences in the USSR school systems, too, arising from local conditions of geography, language, and race. But it is precisely uniformity in the *substance* of education—in the ordering of knowledge, in its orientation and motivation—that is to be feared. A single system of state-supported schools based upon a philosophy in which the ultimate questions of religion and philosophy had been eliminated would impose a unity in American education that would be indistinguishable from totalitarian uniformity.

A democratic state should favor the maximum, not the minimum, of cultural freedom for its citizens. It has the right to establish reasonable standards for voluntary agencies engaged in education, just as it does for groups engaged in social welfare works. But it should encourage voluntary enterprise as much as possible. Here is where our federal social security programs, as well as such private programs as health insurance, show to great advantage. They maximize freedom. The money a person receives from the federal government's old-age insurance policy will indemnify any hospital he prefers to enter, public or private, religious or nonsectarian. This principle of maximizing liberty in the area of social welfare is a sound one. It could well be extended, so that in the case of all services paid by taxes the state (which decides the taxes to be paid) will not dictate what agency must be used in order to share in the common tax benefit.

It is not easy to understand why men in the business world who see red when the state replaces free enterprise by government-run business and warn about "creeping socialism," never raise their voices against what, except for Catholic schools, would be a virtual government monopoly of education. The same wonder arises over the attitude of the medical profession, which vigor-

ously fights proposals to expand government-sponsored medical
services, dubbing these "socialized medicine," but seldom com-
plains about "socialized" education. In the field of education the
Catholic Church, by resisting at enormous price to its members
the trend toward a state monopoly, is leading the fight for democratic freedom of education. And yet for engaging in this struggle
the Church is charged by some with being "undemocratic" and
"un-American."

The privately sponsored, religiously oriented schools are, as we
saw earlier, the oldest schools in the nation. A recent U. S. Office
of Education publication was only making due acknowledgement
in stating that the nonpublic schools of the nation have played
"an enormous role in transmitting our cultural heritage and en-
riching it" and have exerted "a tremendous influence in fashion-
ing the American way of life."[11]

Those modern critics who claim to fear that the existence of
nonpublic schools is somehow a threat to the best interests of
America argue from an assumption that is open to challenge. They
believe that the public school has somehow been elevated to the
status of the "establishment," and, as the official guardian and
interpreter of Americanism, is the natural child of the distinctively Protestant theology of church, state, and freedom enshrined
in the Constitution—which itself has become the absolute norm
by which Catholicism and anything non-Protestant must be
judged. The accusation that after three hundred years the existence of private and parochial schools has somehow sapped the
strength of our democracy is hardly borne out by the evidence.
These critics insinuate that in preserving diversity in social and
cultural opportunities, preferences, and allegiances, these schools
have not been a valuable force in unifying men in political es-
sentials. We might make our own here the quiet reminder of one
of the great legal minds of the last generation:

"The nation is no more preserved by the public school than
it is by the other educational agencies. The Fathers of the Republic and a large proportion of those who from the beginning
were its finest citizens never attended a public school, and even
today a large number of the best exemplars of Americanism have

[11] *The State and Nonpublic Schools* (Misc. No. 28) (Washington, D.C.:
U. S. Government Printing Office, 1958), p. 1.

received and are receiving their education outside of our public schools."[12]

The allegation that parochial school education is divisive has never been documented. When critics are asked to substantiate their "fears," they frequently must fall back on impressions. As a matter of fact, the few sociological surveys that have gone into this subject come up with findings which should help to assuage the critics' fears. "We could find no evidence that parochial schools tend to alienate individual Catholics from their communities," stated the Rossi study. "Parochial school Catholics were as involved in community affairs as anyone else of comparable occupational position."[13]

One non-Catholic student of America's religious divisions, Dr. Leo Pfeffer, has made the observation that "there is in many respects a greater diversity in parochial schools than in public schools." Why?:

> The intentional or de facto zoning which divides neighborhoods into upper class and lower class, Negro and white, Puerto Rican and native in the East, Mexican and native in the Southwest, results in public schools that are largely homogeneous in economic, social and ethnic groupings. Such homogeneity, if not completely absent in parochial schools, is far less prominent. If the children in parochial schools are all of one religion, they are more likely to be of different social, economic, racial and ethnic origins.[14]

They are also likely to have much broader attitudes toward problems of the world community. After all, they are members of a world-wide religious society which is coextensive in time with two thousand years of Western history. As writer Mary McCarthy has shrewdly observed, "If you are born and brought up a Catholic, you have absorbed a good deal of world history and the history of ideas before you are twelve, and it is like learning a language

---

[12] Louis Marshall, for the American Jewish Committee. Amicus Curiae Brief, *Pierce* v. *Society of Sisters*, 268 U. S. 510, 45 Sup. Ct. 571 (1925).

[13] "Background and Consequences of Parochial School Education," Peter H. and Alice S. Rossi, *Harvard Educational Review*, XXVII, 3 (Summer 1957), p. 195.

[14] Leo Pfeffer, *Creeds in Competition* (New York: Harper & Brothers, 1958), p. 81.

early; the effect is indelible. Nobody else in America, no other group, is in this fortunate position."[15]

A Catholic bears the mark of history upon his person. His cultural perspective is broader and deeper than that of his American Protestant neighbor, about whom another student of the contemporary scene has written: "Everything that took place, religiously speaking, before Jamestown, the *Mayflower,* William Penn or Mary Baker Eddy appears to him to be something which happened to foreigners, not to the American Protestant or to anyone he knows."[16]

To anyone who feels that a "ghetto mentality" is necessarily inculcated in Catholic education, the chapter of the Fichter study on "Social Attitudes and Standards" in the parochial school should present challenging reading.[17] The broad liberal and international attitudes of parochial school children in general, however, come as no surprise to those familiar with the atmosphere of these schools.

How "American" are parochial schools? Inordinately—or at least to an embarrassing degree—according to some Catholic educators. The lists of national prize winners in essay and declamation contests on topics of patriotic and civic interest are usually top-heavy with the names of winners and finalists from Catholic schools. Not only do American flags flutter conspicuously in these schools, but in some of them patriotism and citizenship seem to be almost feverishly cultivated. Some 3,200 Good Citizenship clubs in Catholic elementary and junior high school grades took an enthusiastic part in a national citizenship competition sponsored by the Commission on American Citizenship of the Catholic University of America in the spring of 1959. Awards were presented for a variety of activities, such as get-out-the-vote campaigns, studies of government, visits to state legislatures, civic projects, fund raising for community charities, Brotherhood Week, and Constitution Day programs.

Local American Legion, Veterans of Foreign Wars or Catholic

[15] *Memories of a Catholic Girlhood* (New York: Harcourt, Brace and Company, 1957).

[16] Thurston N. Davis, S.J., *America,* August 3, 1957.

[17] Chapter 5 in Joseph H. Fichter, *Parochial School: A Sociological Study* (Notre Dame, Ind.: Univ. of Notre Dame Press, 1958).

War Veterans posts can further document this intense interest by parochial schools in almost anything with a civic or patriotic appeal to it. Perhaps this partially explains the touchiness of many Catholics over doubts cast upon their patriotism. In any event, Catholics have grounds for resentment in the slurring reference to parochial school education as something less American than the public school. As a group the graduates of Catholic schools have had no difficulty fitting into American society. Their loyalty and devotion to the country in war and peace leaves nothing to be desired. On what then is the charge based that the Catholic schools in which so many of these citizens were educated are "a threat to our democratic unity?" Why should the continued growth and prosperity of these schools be feared as inherently divisive of American democracy, any more than, say, synagogues, labor unions, Union League clubs, or Masonic temples?

The charge of divisiveness betrays a serious confusion of thought. The expansion of any rival independent system is, in some measure, made at the expense of the public schools. It can be granted that this situation somewhat affects the good of the present structure of public education. (The obvious remedy here is to modify the structure. As New York's Governor William H. Seward warned in 1842, it is an antidemocratic principle that "society must conform itself to the public schools, instead of the public schools adapting themselves to the exigencies of society.") The good of American society, however, is neither identical nor coextensive with the good of the public schools. The common good of American society has been well served by the public schools, yes, but it would be a case of wagging the puppy by the caudal appendage to forget that service to society is the function of all public institutions. Let there be no confusion about it: the growth of parochial schools conceivably may have affected the well-being of the public schools as they exist today, but the growth of parochial schools has not adversely affected the well-being of the American republic.

Let us push the argument of divisiveness further. If the common good of the American nation hinges on a single uniform type of schooling, then no competing system of schools should be tolerated. It is not the further growth of these schools that should be questioned but the propriety of their existence at all. This is the point to which critics of the growth of nonpublic schools should honestly address themselves. Either nonpublic schools have a right to exist and to multiply freely according to the wishes of their patrons or they do not. If they do not have the right, the state should, at the very most, allow only a few schools of this type to operate in widely separated areas as a symbol of America's traditional tolerance—showcases, on the model of the churches left open in some Communist countries. The number of such schools should be rigorously restricted. Advocates of a state-school monopoly should logically insist on a quota or cut-off point—a percentage beyond which nonpublic schools become a menace.

At present, about 14 per cent of the nation's total elementary and secondary school enrollment is housed in Catholic schools. Many cities, however, have long since surpassed the national figure. In dozens of towns and suburban communities the parochial school enrolls 40, 50, and even in some cases, 60 per cent of the school population. One half the children of Green Bay, Wisconsin, and 52 per cent of the Manchester, New Hampshire, children are in Catholic schools. The Catholic school systems in many of the largest cities of the United States enroll one quarter or more of the total school population. Here are some of the percentages: New York, 26; Chicago, 34; Philadelphia, 39; Detroit, 23. The figure for Hartford is 24 per cent; for Cincinnati, 28; for Boston, 30; for Milwaukee and New Orleans, 33; for Buffalo, 40; for Pittsburgh, 42.[18]

These figures invite reflection. Philosophers of public school education might profitably consider the judgment passed on the American public school by these statistics. Millions of families have shown a preference for another kind of school, although this has meant doubling the cost they must pay for their children's

[18] These figures were kindly furnished to the author by the superintendents of schools in the respective dioceses. This pattern of growth can be expected to continue for one obvious reason. During the past seven years, 30 per cent of the babies born in the nation were baptized into the Catholic Church. This is the national average. In many of the highly populated states the percentage is considerably higher. In Massachusetts and Connecticut over 60 per cent of the total births during 1957 took place in Catholic families. In the same year the Catholic births in New York and New Jersey were 50 per cent of the total, and in Pennsylvania the figure was 40 per cent.

education. There is no present probability of the direct suppression of nonpublic schools. (Without some new form of government support, however, parochial school education may find itself priced out of business—which would be an indirect form of suppression.) Presumably, American society will have to accept the fact that wherever feasible Catholics will continue to build and expand their own school facilities, or that some modification of the present structure of the public school must be made, so that broader Catholic participation could become a possibility. We will return to these choices.

A community has every right to raise the question of the effects of placing a high proportion of its school children in a school or school system separate from the common school. Unless such a school does take measures to overcome the tendency toward separatism, community relations can become painfully strained. On the other hand, Catholics feel that there are other social areas besides the classroom where children from different schools can be encouraged to mingle, as in neighborhood recreational associations and clubs, the scouting movement, shared extracurricular activities, etc. In fact much more could be done along this line by the schools themselves to bring pupils from neighboring schools together. In many cities Catholic school teams join in athletic leagues with public schools; and where they do not, it is usually because they are not welcome. On a local level there are communities where recreational facilities are shared, where exchange assemblies and co-operative projects are the accepted pattern. Much more waits to be done in this area. What more normal a pattern of "togetherness" could there be than the use of the same transportation facilities? Yet, in many states the school bus has been turned into one more divider between the parochial school children and their neighborhood companions who go to the public school.

The factors making for separatism do not all lie on the Catholic side. It is a matter of record that almost every gesture made by Catholic leaders to work out an equitable solution to the school question has been rebuffed. Requests for a fair hearing of the Catholic point of view from the days of Archbishop John Hughes of New York down to modern times have been generally ignored, misinterpreted, or heaped with scorn. Non-Catholics generally have shown little appreciation of the dilemma—moral and financial—that confronts their Catholic fellow citizens. Catholics are not unaware of the values to be gained in the civic and social order by having their children enrolled in the common public school. They want to share in everything American that is good. On the other hand, they appreciate the importance of a religiously centered education which they are convinced cannot be had in the secularized public school. The billions of dollars they have devoted to building and staffing independent schools witness the depth of this conviction. Their attitude results from a philosophy of life, and cannot be dismissed with the query, "Why aren't our public schools good enough for Catholics too?" The Catholic preference for parochial school education is not so much a rejection of the public schools as it is a choice of something qualitatively different. To quote again from the Rossi study, "It would appear that an improvement in the quality of public schools would not materially affect their attractiveness to Catholics, for the greater pull of church schools is based on religious qualities which the public schools have deliberately avoided."[19] This is the dilemma.

The American people have traditionally insisted that the school accept a share of the responsibility for character formation. The emphasis in every period of our history upon the basic moral nature of education has been a reflection of the popular conviction that education is more than teaching children to read, write, and cipher. Today, the consensus is as clear as yesterday that the school is to play a leading part in fitting the child for his destiny, in giving dignity and direction to his life, in preparing him to achieve his end both as an individual and as a member of society.

The history of the American public school has made it painfully apparent that the American people have been caught in an unresolved ambiguity. They insist that the common school assume a certain responsibility for character education, but they do not agree on what should comprise character education. The people have given the common school a moral mandate whose subject is forever in dispute among the different groups served by the school. The central problem is the contradiction inherent in the

[19] "Background and Consequences of Parochial School Education," pp. 195–96.

very idea of one common school attempting to serve a religiously pluralistic society. Correlative to this problem, of course, is the place of the independent, church-related school in the total scheme of things. The coexistence within the same society of groups holding fundamental differences regarding the nature and destiny of man makes for an impasse in the approach to the moral side of education. Values of an ethical and moral order must be rooted in that to which men give ultimate importance in life. It is plain that only in a society in which men agree on the substance of ultimate values can there be an acceptable program for character training. Were the American community homogeneous in religious faith, the public school might quite properly give religious instruction in the common school.

For a long time in American history there was some basis for a general agreement on values and their sanctions. The Old World inheritance of Greco-Roman natural law and of many of the central religious concepts of the Judeo-Christian tradition was universally accepted and widely operative in our early, Protestant-dominated American society. Though there were important differences between the Dutch Calvinists and the French Huguenots, between the Swedish Lutherans and the German Reformed Lutherans, or among the English Puritans, Quakers, and Anglicans who colonized America, all of these different peoples were bound together by a common Christian tradition and their "protest" against the Mother Church of Rome. Though community tensions often did arise from the dogmatic, linguistic and national differences separating these pioneer groups, there remained always a core of ethical values and religious beliefs derived from a common source.

Agreement, at least on the basis and general content of a philosophy of character education for the common public school, was then more possible than now. Today, belief in God, the understanding of the nature of divinity and of the implications of religious belief for conduct run to every shade of the spectrum. For the traditional orthodox believer, God is still an absolute, eternal, transcendent, personal—and for Christians, triune—Being. Yet each of these attributes is the occasion for religious division, separating groups of Americans into different sects. Today, the public school serves children who come to it from families divided into more than 250 different religious bodies. This is pluralism with a vengeance.

One solution to the problem of religion in the public school is that of those who argue that there are certain commonly held essential truths in religion, such as the being of God, the revelation of the divine will in the Bible, the voice of conscience, and a future life. Because these truths are the bedrock of the religion of all God-fearing men and women, it is argued, they should be part of public school instruction and training. When more closely examined, this solution amounts only to the setting up of a new religious sect and adding one more denomination to the long list. For religion cannot exist in an undenominational form. Even the basic doctrine of God's existence carries with it a determined concept of what God is. The finite deities of the animists, for example, have nothing in common with the infinite deity of Eastern Asia and the Old Testament. Brahmanism conceives its god as the negation of all divine attributes, and Aristotle's god was Pure Act containing all perfection. Pantheism is at the opposite pole to the monotheistic Jehovah-God of the Bible, who is self-determined and personal and transcends nature. Mere deism, on the other hand, since it denies the possibility of certain belief, flatly contradicts all creeds. The actual teaching of a living religion in the schools, therefore, cannot avoid taking a denominational form, and, moreover, this "common-denominator" religion must derive its validity from some authority—reason, intuition, faith, tradition, revelation, or some combination of these.

Advocates of the common-denominator approach are continually frustrated by the courts, which are under the necessity of defending the religious freedom and the rights of conscience of all citizens in the state's common schools. Since all state constitutions forbid the teaching of any doctrine favorable to a single sect or distinctive of any religious group, this renders it legally impossible to keep religion in any traditional form in the schools. No religious belief or moral practice of one group in society is then free from legal challenge by another group. If, for example, sect A believes in a trinitarian God, the contradictory belief of sect B (which holds for a unitarian divinity) cancels out belief in a triune God. The same holds for any other religious proposition, whether it relates to the resurrection and miracles of Jesus Christ, the nature of the church and its government, or the reality of death, judgment, and other divine sanctions.

This is even more the case with ethical patterns which involve social behavior. Marriage, divorce, birth control, gambling, drinking, blood transfusions, vaccination, nudity, flag saluting, military service have all, at one time or another in recent years, been defended or attacked in the name of religion. The affirmation of one of these beliefs or ethical practices could be an affront to any group holding the contradictory position. In court test after court test, the decision handed down has been in favor of the dissident group—to save them from real or fancied invasions of their religious liberty. This is part of the price we pay for our religious pluralism.

But even if there were an inoffensive nonsectarian religion that could be taught in the common school, from the family's point of view what has been gained? No Catholic parent is really satisfied when his children are merely *not* being educated in a belief contrary to his own. It is normal to assume that he wants them brought up to believe that what he holds is important truth. Orestes Brownson long ago said, "I always hold that to be important truth, wherein I differ from others." He meant that if differences were inconsequential, there would be no point in being different. It is precisely the conviction that a doctrinal difference is important that keeps the sincere churchgoer in a Methodist rather than an Episcopalian or Catholic pew. The compromise approach, whose great patron, as we saw, was Horace Mann, contained the principle of its own dissolution. The precious little common ground that once existed among Unitarians, Methodists, Congregationalists, Jews, Catholics, and deists gradually was eroded away.

The positive doctrinal elements regarding church organization, sacraments, and the mission of Christ had to be strained out of the common school piece by piece to avoid offending dissenters. This process played right into the hands of groups holding a minimum of positive doctrine. A blandly Christian flavor that contented Unitarians and Universalists could only dismay Congregationalists and Episcopalians. In time the soup got so thin that it pleased no palate. Belief in God, the Golden Rule, and the Bible were about all that survived this disintegrating process.

The Bible in the classroom later became an object of contention between Protestants and Catholics with the result that the courts have banned Bible reading in many states. Belief in God has until recent years fared better, but a number of communities have had to impose silence even on this point upon their schools. In September 1956, for example, New York City public school officials and their lay advisers found considerable opposition to a policy statement on values that contained preferential references to God and belief in God, and had to delete several references to these ideas in the final form of the statement on moral and spiritual values.[20] In January 1959 Chicago's Parent-Teacher Association recorded its formal opposition to any teaching about God in the city's public schools. Such instruction, the P.T.A. statement said, was the responsibility of parents and churches. "We firmly believe," it went on, "that no public school system should be used to aid any or all religious faiths or sects in the dissemination of their doctrines and ideals."

Uncritical allegiance to the principle that religious freedom in a religiously divided community requires the elimination of any teaching or practice from the public school not acceptable to the entire community has made it impossible to preserve any kind of traditional religion in the schools. The shadowy, moralistic, natural substitute for traditional religion that does survive in the schools, optimistically called "moral and spiritual values," might as well be based on the Koran, the Vedas, or the Tables of Confucius.

There is another well-intentioned and commonly heard solution to the religious question. It begins with the assumption that the public school can lay a foundation for character—if not general Protestant Christianity, at least basic natural law morality—upon which other educative agencies in society can build. Underlying this assumption, however, is a theory of religion and religious commitment which is not compatible with the Catholic understanding of these things. Hence, it is impossible for Catholics to be fully

[20] See Neil G. McCluskey, S.J., "Spiritual Values in Public Schools," *America*, September 29, 1956.

satisfied with statements of moral and spiritual values which make claim to supply such a foundation.

What we consider popularly as the three great American faiths —Protestantism, Catholicism, Judaism—are not simply variations of a single basic theistic philosophy. The prophetic and individualistic genius of Protestantism runs counter to the authoritative institutionalized character of Catholicism; whereas the communal and ritualistic spirit of Judaism places it apart from either Protestant or Catholic Christianity. Granted that there are certain common positions among the three groups which conceivably could provide a basis for a common value philosophy, universal acknowledgement of them is lacking.

Nonetheless, in the years since World War II a large number of educators have urged that since natural law theism was the basis of our original political consensus and is still commonly accepted, it should be reaffirmed as the basis for a common program of moral and spiritual values in the public school. When Catholics support this position, it is not at all because it satisfies the Catholic ideal. It is simply that they consider this minimum better than nothing at all. For the symbolism in our schools even of natural law theism does have positive values. It does testify to our continuity with the religious tradition of the Founding Fathers. It does reaffirm the basis of the American public philosophy. It does serve to remind the impressionable child of some fundamental natural truths. It does throw up a barrier against the constant pressure of those minorities who seek the further secularization of the public schools.

Catholics deplore the tensions which periodically arise from religious differences. They have a duty, as have all other American citizens, to avoid what will needlessly give offense, to seek opportunities to build up community understanding and, in general, to work for civic harmony. They are, though, more aware than most of their non-Catholic neighbors that ever since Cain broke with his family and went off on his own, the human race has been plagued by some sort of religious pluralism. The unity of the human family has been weakened in every generation by disagreements and divisions over religion, and a basic problem of each generation has been to find a way of living together without that primordial unity which once bound man to man, and mankind to God.

It is not easy to visualize the compromises that would be necessary before Catholic citizens could come to accept the public school as fully their own. This much, however, is certain. Catholic citizens cannot modify any religious convictions in order to achieve greater acceptance as "Americans" in the full community. Even if Catholics could modify their convictions on the nature of education to achieve this result, the price would be too great. Cultural and religious pluralism means at least the freedom to preserve differences. The day that such freedom disappears, the nation that came into being in 1776 will also have disappeared.

CHAPTER 3

The Evolution of the Secular School

By the beginning of this century, public education had moved far from the nonsectarian compromise devised by earlier educators to preserve the commonly held truths of Protestant Christianity. The first schools, as we have seen, even when supported fully by community funds, retained their distinctive religious orientation. The nonsectarian, biblically based, liberal Protestantism in the schools was an uneasy and temporary truce. The continued fragmentation of the Protestant churches dramatized differences over dogma, both among the Protestant majority and with the Catholic group whose numbers now gave them a greater voice in the community. An influential school of educators came to the fore with a philosophy of education which insisted that, since religious education was incompatible with secular learning, the two must be handled separately. An even more influential group, whose ultimate values derived from a secular and humanist rather than a Christian tradition, argued that in a democratic age enlightened by science belief in a supernaturalist religion was an anachronism. Given the religious pluralism of American society, it only required the confluence of these two streams of thought to bring about a general policy of separating all religion and religiously oriented character education from the public school.

The First Amendment—one of the ten adopted simultaneously with the Federal Constitution to spell out the American Bill of Rights—did recognize the pluralistic religious structure of the new states. Though in 1787, the year of the Constitutional Convention, all of the New England states (except Rhode Island), Maryland,

and South Carolina still had established churches, no church was to have a preferred status as the *nationally* established one. Nor was the government to curtail the free exercise of religion. In applying these principles of the First Amendment to the schools, men argued that respect for liberty of conscience required that sectarian religious instruction be kept out of the schools. Though the interests of the Protestant churches and sects in the common schools were, in theory at least, still protected, the interests of non-Protestants were not. The religious education program was symbolized by the reading of "neutral" passages of the Bible, generally ethical rather than dogmatic in emphasis. But for Catholics, reading the King James Bible, like reciting the "Protestant" Lord's Prayer—both compulsory practices in the schools—was anathema. Far more was at stake here than some variant readings of minor literary importance or the exact canonical ordering of the books of the Bible. These things were symbols of the fundamental cleavage of Christendom, and around these two symbols Protestant and Catholic rallied as to a battle standard.

Since Catholics took strong exception to the Protestant bias in the common schools, they were left with two alternatives. They could work to eliminate all traces of the Protestant religion from the schools, or they could withdraw their children and place them in schools of their own. Catholic requests for a share in the school-tax fund were, with few exceptions, rejected outright, so that Catholic parents were thrown back on their own resources. The Catholic Church of the nineteenth and early twentieth centuries was largely the church of the laboring immigrant class whose financial resources could not be stretched to cover the great need. Since there were never enough parochial schools to accommodate Catholic children, Catholic energy in many communities was expended on de-Protestantizing the common schools. Catholic pressure, then, was partially responsible for forcing formalized religion out of the schools and ensuring a broader neutrality toward all institutionalized religion. There were, nonetheless, other equally important factors involved, some of which already have been discussed.

The transcendentalist views of life and reality, elegantly publicized in the writings of men like Ralph Waldo Emerson and Amos Bronson Alcott, helped put religion and morals on a broader "nonsectarian" basis. The American people, though not yet ready to tolerate a fully secular philosophy based upon science and naturalism, did respond, as one historian has put it, "to a generalized religious outlook of love, beneficence, and moral virtue that was divorced from specific sectarian creeds but not divorced from Christian idealism in general."[1]

About this same time important voices in the educational world were making acceptable the idea that by its very nature the school is completely secular and hence incompetent to enter the area of religious education. This position was not dictated by hostility toward religion or religious values in education, nor did it question the importance of religion in life. It was rather concerned with the most fitting occasion for efficient instruction in religion and with safeguarding the rights of private conscience. This policy, in turn, was considered a postulate of the constitutional separation of church and state.

This was the position Cardinal Gibbons referred to, when he wrote Pope Leo XIII in 1890, explaining that the absence of religious education in American public schools was not due to opposition to religion as in France and Italy. "The public spirit in this country," he wrote, "is fundamentally religious, and there is everywhere a great respect for liberty of conscience well understood and in the legitimate sense of the word."[2] However, the religious question had been set aside in the schools, he explained, in order not to offend the sentiments of the children and their parents, and the care of providing the religious education of the children was left to the Church and the Protestant sects.

Among the highly influential men who advanced this separatist philosophy was William Torrey Harris, superintendent of schools in St. Louis between 1868 and 1880, and U. S. Commissioner of Education from 1889 to 1906. A devout man himself, Harris favored religious education but only in what he considered its proper place, the church. He held that in method, spirit, and content secular truth was necessarily antagonistic to the acquisition of religious truth, so much so that the two could not be taught under the same roof. Religious instruction was the prerogative of the

---

[1] R. Freeman Butts and Lawrence A. Cremin, *A History of Education in American Culture* (New York: Henry Holt and Co., 1953), p. 170.
[2] Ellis, p. 664.

church. To farm it out to the secular school would be, in the nature
of things, to let it degenerate into "mere deism bereft of a living
Providence, or else changing the school into a parochial school
and destroying the efficiency of secular instruction."[3]

The men who propagated these views argued that the responsibility for the education of the child must be shared by all the great
institutions of society. It was a mistake to thrust upon the public
school the charge for the child's complete training, and ignore
the education furnished by the family, the church, and the community. It was just as great a mistake to take education completely
out of the state's hands in favor of parochial schools, on the score
that religious education was inseparable from secular education.
Such a policy flouted the great lesson of history that the separation
of church and state is the surest safeguard of individual liberty.
Freedom for everyone to follow the dictates of conscience was
the cornerstone of republican institutions, and these could never
flourish except upon the conviction that the secular by itself was
worthy of great respect. Where this respect had been lost, republican institutions were the loser. The public school system
should be regulated by the sincere desire to respect the feelings
and wishes of all citizens. Let the community see to it that the
schools are free from sectarian bias of every kind, and then the
church, through its appropriate instrumentalities, will best perform its mission.

This is the philosophy of education recognizable in the 1947
decision of the U. S. Supreme Court in the Everson school bus
case. "Our public school," wrote Justice Robert H. Jackson,
". . . is organized on the premise that secular education can be
isolated from all religious teaching so that the school can inculcate
all needed temporal knowledge and also maintain a strict neutrality as to religion."

An even more important contemporary witness that this concept is part of the philosophy governing our public schools may
be found in these lines from the NEA Educational Policies Commission statement of 1951:

---

[3] Harris is one of the most overlooked figures in American education. Yet
few men have equaled his influence. See the author's *Public Schools and
Moral Education*, pp. 99–176.

The teaching of moral and spiritual values in the public schools of the United States must be done without endangering religious freedom and without circumventing the policy of separation of Church and state. Our society leaves to the home and the church the responsibility for instruction designed to secure the acceptance of a religious faith. Thus the home, the church, and the school each share in moral and spiritual development, while each may make the contribution to that development for which it is peculiarly fitted.[4]

The 1951 document listed ten basic moral and spiritual values which are accepted by most Americans, though there are wide differences of opinion relative to the reasons for approval or sanction. The basic values are the supreme importance of the individual personality, the moral responsibility of each individual, institutions as the servants of men, common consent, devotion to truth, respect for excellence, moral equality, brotherhood, the pursuit of happiness, and spiritual enrichment.

During an earlier period of our history these moral and spiritual values were universally assumed to be based upon traditional religious value-systems; for example, there was no ambiguity about the theistic bias of documents like the Northwest Ordinance of 1787 and the Southwest Ordinance of 1790. The framers of these and similar laws could assume universal acceptance by the nation of a theistically based natural law upon which was reared the unity of what men considered a "Christian" nation. This included belief in the existence of a Creator who was the source of the justice and the rights defined in the nation's first great political documents. Consequently, the educational philosophy of American educators then included many concepts of natural law theism and divine sanctions, which would no longer find universal acceptance. This change has seriously complicated the modern approach to character education in the public schools. No longer can agreement be assumed concerning a theistic basis—a belief in God—for statements on moral and spiritual values in the common school. Increasingly it happens that when the attempt is made to formu-

[4] National Education Association and American Association of School Administrators, Educational Policies Commission, *Moral and Spiritual Values in the Public Schools* (Washington: The Commission, 1951), p. 6.

late such a statement by a majority in a community, many groups will no longer give assent.

It would be an oversimplification, however, and like every oversimplification, unfair to the reality, to lump all dissenting groups together as atheists or even "secularists" as the word is applied to scientific humanists or ethical culturists. Many, who do not accept moral and spiritual value statements built on belief in God, dissent upon other grounds. Some dissenters feel that such statements infringe upon the freedom of conscience of non-Christians and non-believers. Others claim to be following out the principle that the school's competence does not extend beyond secular subjects. This does not mean, both groups would maintain, that the school atmosphere should be hostile to religion or religious values. The NEA Educational Policies Commission statement, for instance, expressly warned that the school should in no way "bring the constructive moral or religious teaching of the home into contempt or disrepute." Moreover, the document said, "A good teacher will not shrug aside the religious convictions of children and their parents as being unimportant or 'unscientific.'"

Secular learning, according to these groups, should be communicated in an atmosphere in which proper emphasis is placed upon moral and spiritual values, and this appreciation should be a normal result of the educative process. Religious values or religious training itself, however, must be attended to outside the school. Again, fundamental to this position is the principle that the development of moral habits in the school somehow lays the groundwork for religious education. By inculcating a basis of moral discipline and spiritual attitudes the public school prepares the child to receive the superstructure of religious training from home and church.

Horace Mann and William Torrey Harris represented some of the best educational thought of their times in proceeding on the assumption that the common school could lay such a foundation for character. In the case of Mann it was general Protestant Christianity; in the case of Harris it was basic natural law morality. The same assumption is widely operative today, but is one which Catholics have great difficulty in reconciling with their own philosophy of education. The theory of religion and religious commitment beneath this assumption likewise causes trouble for the Jewish conscience.

The intrinsic limitations imposed upon the common school by the religiously pluralistic structure of our society would, in any event, have made the problem of religion in the public schools a difficult one to solve. On the other hand, though, the problem of religious pluralism has been solved in similar areas of government activity, for example, in the provision for chaplains in the armed forces, and in state hospitals and prisons. Again, had the Catholic parent only to work out some kind of compromise with his non-Catholic neighbors holding a philosophy of education based on the simple separation of religious and secular learning, good will and ingenuity might have come up with compromises that would have gone a long way toward resolving the problem. There is a third factor, however, that has rendered the problem of religion in public education impossible of solution from the Catholic point of view.

The national policy of excluding religion, at least in the traditional sense, from the American public school is the secularist philosophy that is more and more dominating public education. Known under various designations—scientific humanism, social psychologism, ethical culturism, personalism, pragmatism, instrumentalism, or perhaps what best describes it, democratic humanism—it is the most influential philosophy in the great teachers colleges and schools of education from Columbia University in New York to the University of California on the Pacific coast. Some notion of this domination can be gained when it is realized that in these institutions are trained a very high proportion of the men and women who staff the teacher-training schools, who become the professional educators in the federal and state Offices of Education, who are the leaders and spokesmen for national educational groups, and who fill the overwhelming majority of the administrative posts in the public school systems of the nation.

Many prominent educators have been closely identified with modern philosophies of secularism which vary only in accidentals. Their names include those of Alexander Meiklejohn and Max Carl Otto of the University of Wisconsin, Boyd H. Bode of Ohio State University, Felix Adler who founded the Ethical Culture

Movement, and William O. Stanley of the University of Illinois. But the great source of the current secularist philosophy of education has been Columbia University and its Teachers College. Here, several generations of American educators learned the nature of education at the feet of William Heard Kilpatrick, John L. Childs, George S. Counts, Harold Rugg, Goodwin Watson, and John Dewey—men who for nearly fifty years expounded the theory today governing moral education in our American public schools.

The ideas of these men on religion and morality are literally worlds apart from the Christian tradition. The contrast is between the natural and the supernatural, between this world of space and time and the realm of the eternal attained through faith. The differences do not lie in the accidental order but concern the very substance of religion and morality. Here is no question of a few doctrinal modifications to be made in order to liberalize religious belief. These men seek an end to traditional religion, because they look upon it as something essentially incompatible with modern science, as something harmful to the best interests of society, and therefore something to be eradicated from the schools of a democracy.

To anyone who may think that agreement or compromise is possible between the Christian and secularist understanding of ultimate values, John Dewey himself addresses these words of warning:

> The opposition between religious values as I conceive them and religions is not to be bridged. Just because the release of these values is so important, their identification with the creeds and cults of religions must be dissolved.[5]

This sweeping rejection of all historic religions—Protestant and Catholic, orthodox and liberal, traditional and modern, Eastern and Western—is necessary, on secularist premises, to achieve Dewey's goal of "the emancipation of the religious from religion." Most secularists set great store by many of the values upheld in traditional religious faith but they deplore the identification of these with formalized religions. Religious values are, for the

[5] *A Common Faith* (New Haven: Yale Univ. Press, 1934), pp. 27–28.

secularists, located in the unfolding process of natural evolution, and science is their guarantee.

Traditional religions have built their aims, ideals, goods, and values upon the existence of a God—usually a personal God—who transcends empirical experience. The secularist faith offers instead "a vitalized appreciation of the cosmic evolutionary process that can be projected as an aim to be realized." This new religion of humanity is the scientific living of social democracy in an industrial age whose highest value is the "shared experience of democratic living." Civic and social values are substituted for traditional moral and religious values. The virtues to be held aloft in the schools are civic and social. The energies of religious devotion and dedication are no longer to be wasted in preparing for "another" life but are to be expended in ameliorating the conditions of society as it exists now. Belief in a transcendent personal deity gives way to belief in the blending of ideal and actual humanity which is evolving from and continuous with those mysterious forces of rationality, beauty, and goodness that are nature's own. What the pre-science age had long regarded as distinctively religious values are actually inherent in natural experience and so discoverable in nature alone. Sociality toward man and piety toward nature adequately cover man's religious experience.

A lucid exposition of the central point of the Deweyan religion of nature is given by Sidney Hook, distinguished interpreter and collaborator of John Dewey:

> Dewey believes that it is possible to have a sense of dependence upon, and humility before, the cosmic forces on which we must rely even when we build shelters against them, without surrendering to supernaturalism or to the simple negativism of village *atheism*. Supernaturalism as a creed is hard to accept for a person of intelligence and courage; atheism as a doctrine isolates man from those relations of the physical world which support human achievement. *Natural piety recognizes the continuity between man and nature.* It acknowledges man's kinship of origin, but not of interest or aim, with other living things."[6]

Dewey and the professors who today propagate his ideas about

[6] *John Dewey: An Intellectual Portrait* (New York: John Day Co., 1939), pp. 213–14.

religion and morality appeal to science as their authority. They
claim that they alone are facing the full intellectual scope of the
change in the idea of the universe and of man's history, and hence
have "no alternative but surrender of the older conception of God"
or the broadening of it to meet the challenge of scientific evolu-
tionism. Science has worked a "revolution in the seat of authority."
New scientific methods of inquiry and reflection must be for today's educated man "the final arbiter of all questions of fact,
existence, and intellectual assent."

Some notion of the gulf dividing the religion of secularism from
traditional faiths can be gained by reading John Dewey's "Credo,"
printed in 1930 and reprinted many times since. Here are some
of its basic affirmations and denials:

> It is assumed that Christianity is the final religion; Jesus the
> complete and unchanging embodiment of the divine and the
> human.
> Faith in the divine author and authority in which Western
> civilization confided, inherited ideas of the soul and its destiny,
> of fixed revelation, of completely stable institutions, of auto-
> matic progress, have been made impossible for the cultivated
> mind of the Western world.
> Does renunciation of the extra-empirical compel also an
> abandonment of all religion? It certainly exacts a surrender of
> that supernaturalism and fixed dogma and rigid institutionalism
> with which Christianity has been historically associated.
> Faith in its newer sense signifies that experience itself is the
> sole ultimate authority.
> Religions have been saturated with the supernatural—and the
> supernatural signifies precisely that which lies beyond ex-
> perience.
> Moral codes have been allied to this religious supernaturalism
> and have sought their foundation and sanction in it.
> Contrast with such ideas, deeply imbedded in all Western
> culture, gives the philosophy of faith in experience a definite
> and profound meaning.[7]

[7] *Forum*, LXXXIII (March, 1930), 176–82. A revision of "Credo" was
published in 1939 as part of a larger work, *I Believe*, ed. by Clifton Fadiman
(New York: Simon and Schuster), pp. 347–54.

The adherents of doctrinaire secularism have worked diligently to loosen the hold of traditional religion upon American culture, particularly in the schools. The public schools, in their eyes, are to serve as the particular instruments in promoting the secular ideology. The secularists have attacked faith as outmoded, moral intuition as unscientific, and biblical or church authority as anti-social and undemocratic. They have argued that the historic influence of religions has often been to magnify doctrines which are not subject to critical inquiry and test, thereby nullifying, in effect, the work of the schools. It is not this or that particular item of belief but the attitude engendered by religion to which they object—the cumulative effect of religious doctrines "in producing habits of mind at odds with the attitudes required for maintenance of democracy." Very many social psychologists and philosophers of education have accepted the Deweyan judgment that any philosophy which "glorifies the gulf between the 'material' and the 'spiritual,' between immutable principles and social conditions in a state of rapid change" is the great obstacle impeding the scientific approach to the proper teaching of morals.

John Dewey himself complained: "I cannot understand how any realization of the democratic ideal as a vital moral and spiritual ideal in human affairs is possible without surrender of the conception of the basic division to which supernatural Christianity is committed."[8] The public school has the task and the opportunity of helping to break down "the philosophy of fixation that bolsters external authority in opposition to free co-operation." Furthermore, the school

> must help banish the conception that the daily work and vocation of man are negligible in comparison with literary pursuits, and that human destiny here and now is of slight importance in comparison with some supernatural destiny. It must accept wholeheartedly the scientific way, not merely of technology, but of life in order to achieve the promise of modern democratic ideals.[9]

The reconstruction of the church along secular scientific lines

[8] *A Common Faith*, p. 84.
[9] "Challenge to Liberal Thought," in *Problems of Men* (New York: Philosophical Library, 1946), p. 159.

is the concern of the whole community, though the responsibility for initiating reform belongs primarily to those within the churches. On the other hand, it is the whole community that bears the primary responsibility for conducting the development and the reconstruction of other educational agencies, the public school in particular. The leadership in this movement, however, should belong to those who, "having become conscious in some degree of the modern ideas of nature, of man and society," are best able, consequently, "to forecast the direction which social changes are taking." In other words, the secularists must direct the philosophy of public education. They are to labor persistently and patiently for the clarification and development of "the positive creed of life implicit in democracy and in science, and to work for the transformation of all practical instrumentalities of education till they are in harmony with these ideas."

The secularist strategy for converting public school education called for proper timing. John Dewey urged delaying tactics until the opportune hour should arrive.

"It is lucidity, sincerity, and the sense of reality which demand that, until the non-supernatural view is more completely elaborated in all its implications and is more completely in possession of the machinery of education, the schools shall keep hands off and shall do as little as possible." This is indeed a *laissez-faire* policy. It is frankly, avowedly so. From the secularist point of view this was only wisdom. Until secularist views should be in firmer possession "it is better that our schools should do nothing than that they should do wrong things." Yes, better is it for the schools to confine themselves to their obviously urgent tasks than that they should "under the name of spiritual culture, form habits of mind which are at war with the habits of mind congruous with democracy and with science." This is not laziness or cynicism; "it is honesty, courage, sobriety, and faith."[10] It is, above all, frankness.

Secularist educators have adopted the language of the churches with skillful effect. It is consoling for families with religious backgrounds to be blandly assured that in promoting social unity the

[10] These quotations are from a lengthy article which is the classical statement of John Dewey on the question: "Religion and Our Schools," *Hibbert Journal*, VI (July 1908), 799.

common schools are achieving a genuine religious unity. It is good to know that in assimilating children of different nationalities, languages, traditions, and creeds upon the basis of what is common and public in American endeavor, the public schools are performing an infinitely significant religious work. It is encouraging to read that in some dim but effective way the American public is already conscious that its schools serve best the cause of religion in serving the "cause of social unification"; and that under certain conditions schools are "more religious in substance and in promise without any of the conventional badges and machinery of religious instruction than they could be in cultivating these forms at the expense of state-consciousness." The religion meant here, of course, is the secularist faith in humanity itself as dynamically evolving in American democratic society, and has nothing to do with religion in the time-honored sense.

Several generations of Americans whose approaches to the problem of religion in the common public school have been neutralized by their conflicting pluralist backgrounds have stood by and uneasily watched these ideas take deep root, acquire respectability, and spread widely in the education world. The secularist philosophers of education—many of them disciples of John Dewey —have taught the school people of the United States that all ethical and moral values originate in society. Ultimate moral motives and forces are "nothing more or less than social intelligence— the power of observing and comprehending social situations, and social power—trained capacities of control—at work in the service of social interest and aim."

As a consequence, the moral responsibility of the school, and of those who conduct it, is to society. "Apart from the thought of participation in social life," wrote Dewey, "the school has no end nor aim." In fact, "we get no moral ideas, no moral standards for school life excepting as we so interpret in social terms."[11] *My Pedagogic Creed,* which first appeared in 1897 and was most recently reprinted in 1939 by the National Education Association, helped popularize among America's public school teachers the secularist idea of morality as something essentially social. From its opening sentence—"I believe that all education proceeds by the

[11] "Ethical Principles Underlying Education," in National Herbart Society, *Third Yearbook, 1897,* p. 12.

participation of the individual in the social consciousness of the race"—to its concluding statement seventeen pages later—"In this way the teacher always is the prophet of the true God and the usherer in of the true kingdom of God"—society is held up as the origin and final goal of all mankind's values.

The triumph of thousands of years of human interaction is the emergence of the democratic state. The United States became a nation under historical conditions, according to the Deweyan philosophy, which "enabled it to share in and to appropriate the idea that the state life, the vitality of the social whole, is of more importance than the flourishing of any segment or class." Judged by this principle, any schools which inculcate a different hierarchy of values would certainly be a foreign body in the life stream of the nation. Here is the basic clash between Catholicism and secularism. Here are the roots of secularist opposition to religious education.

Dewey was either more candid in exposing his premises or more intelligent in grasping them than are many of his followers today. Dewey scoffed at the euphemism "separation of church and state" and boldly called it by its true secularist name:

> Doubtless many of our ancestors would have been somewhat shocked to realize the full logic of their own attitude with respect to the subordination of churches to the state (falsely termed the separation of Church and state); but the state idea was inherently of such vitality and constructive force as to carry the practical result, with or without conscious perception of its philosophy.[12]

It is safe conjecture, but still only conjecture, to speculate over the "shock" of nineteenth-century Americans at this interpretation. There is no doubt, however, that in the years since World War II, the American people have risen up in alarm over the inroads secularism has made on the public schools. Charles Clayton Morrison, while editor of the *Christian Century*, was voicing the sentiments of many religious leaders when he wrote:

> Protestantism has been greatly weakened in its inner character by this kind of education. Unlike Catholicism, the Protestant

[12] "Religion and Our Schools," p. 801.

churches . . . have given to the public school their consistent and unreserved devotion. The result is that their own children have been delivered back to their churches with a mentality which is not only unintelligent about religion but relatively incapacitated even to ask the questions out of which religion arises, to say nothing of answering them the way religion answers them.[13]

The mentality of the entire body of American Protestantism, he claimed, has thus been fashioned under the influence of the secularized public school.

Methodist Bishop Fred Peirce Corson went further, stating: "Today the public school is not only ceasing to be a colleague in religious teaching and training, but by its attitude of exclusion, as well as separation, and its renunciation of responsibility, it is becoming an obstacle in the way of adequate religious education."[14]

While the churches remained aloof and were enforcing a strict neutrality upon one another, the missionaries of the secular religion of democracy were not so inhibited in their activity. One Protestant leader has made the astute observation: "The fact that this kind of approach is not connected with any of the traditional Churches means that it can be presented in schools without being spotted as religious teaching that raises Church-state problems."[15] And it was a professor of philosophy at Columbia University's Teachers College, now dean of Carlton College, who frankly stated: "It seems unfortunately to be the case that what has been presented as a means for preserving religious peace and freedom through secularization has to some extent become a method of propagating a particular dogmatic faith, namely, scientific naturalism or, to give it another name, naturalistic humanism."[16]

The reluctance of many people, Catholics as well as non-Catholics, to show enthusiasm for definitions of moral and spiritual values, like this one from the 1951 NEA statement on values—"those values which, when applied in human behavior, exalt and

---

[13] *Christian Century*, April 17, 1946.

[14] *Vital Speeches*, December 19, 1949, p. 146.

[15] John C. Bennett, *Christians and the State* (New York: Charles Scribner's Sons, 1958), p. 238.

[16] Philip H. Phenix, "Religion in American Public Education," *Teachers College Record*, October 1955, p. 30.

refine life and bring it into accord with the standards of conduct that are approved in our democratic culture"—becomes understandable against the foregoing background. This 1951 document lists only sanctions of the natural order for its moral and spiritual values and expressly warns that religious sanctions "may not be explicitly invoked in the public school classroom," adding that "of course they may play a powerful role in the moral and spiritual instruction of home and church." Again, from a Catholic point of view at least, this effort to compromise has put the public school on the side of the ethical scientists and scientific humanists. Moral sanctions which are limited to the secular order and may not be related to religious values necessarily limit character education in the public schools to the purely secular order.

The problem of the Catholic parent and pastor has been compounded by the intransigent attitude of the secularists in everything that touches the question of relating public education to religion. These are the same people who have led the fight against programs of released time and dismissed time for religious instruction, and have made it next to impossible for the public schools to co-operate with the churches in the community. This campaign has been waged ostensibly in the name of religious freedom—protected by our traditional separation between church and state.

Now there is no legitimate quarrel with the constitutional principle of carefully distinguishing the spheres of civil and ecclesiastical authority and respecting the autonomy of each, as we shall discuss in later detail. And yet the ritualistic phrase "absolute separation of church and state" has been used with telling effect in campaigns to eliminate every trace of religion from the public schools.

It is increasingly evident that, even after a century and more of experimenting, the problem of character education in the common public school is more defiant of solution than ever—is, in fact, insoluble. The public school is less competent today to assume responsibility for moral and spiritual training than ever before.

Consider this dilemma. A Catholic starts with an assumption that religion is the central concern of human existence. A Catholic believes that his purpose in life is to learn to live in such a way as to prepare himself for an immortal supernatural destiny. He believes further that God has given him the Church, a visible society functioning in the temporal world, in order to assist him to attain an eternal objective which transcends this world.

Today, any philosophy of education presenting such a goal is constrained to operate outside the public schools. Faced with the ultimate question of whether religion is the starting point and essence of true education, the public school has had to adopt a theoretical neutrality between those who believe in the God of the Western tradition and those who do not. Yet, the public school, in a Catholic analysis, is not really neutral, for it gives an equivalent denial to the questions by actually taking another starting point and aiming at another goal. What is worse, by default the public school facilitates the entry of a naturalist religion of democracy, or secularist cult of society, into the vacuum, so that only the child from a secularist home can feel perfectly at home in the common public school. By default, civic or political virtue has become the primary goal of public school education. In other words, these schools must exist primarily to produce good citizens.

There are those who believe the perfection of the temporal social order to be the supreme and ultimate aim of life; they have no quarrel with this interpretation of the public school's responsibility for character education. There are those who, while believing in a supernatural dimension to education and life, see here no irresolvable conflict of value-systems; they too give allegiance to the public school. But there are those believers in a supernatural—including Catholics—who do see an irresolvable conflict here; they cannot give their unqualified allegiance.

The conclusion is inescapable. We can prescind here from the theoretical question as to whether the public school could ever, under any circumstances, adequately care for the moral side of a Catholic child's education. We do say that the system as presently constituted is simply incapable of doing so. This conclusion haunts the overwhelming majority of Catholic parents to the point that they are almost desperate in their desire to have their youngsters in Catholic schools.

CHAPTER 4

The Catholic School in Theory

To some observers the Catholic school may well appear to be a carbon copy of the neighboring public school.[1] The basic objectives, organization, curriculum, standards, activities, and educational results, at a casual glance, seem pretty much the same. They know, of course, that some provision is made in the Catholic school for religious instruction. They know that there is different ownership and control. But apart from these obvious differences they fail to see anything essential that distinguishes the Catholic school from the public school. Accordingly, they are hard put to account for the enormous sacrifice on the part of Catholic parents, pastors, and teachers in building and operating a separate school system and they cannot understand why Catholics generally regard the public school as unsuitable for the education of their children.

On the other hand, some people picture the Catholic school as a kind of all-week Sunday school, in which the pupils are drilled in the catechism by nuns from nine in the morning until three in the afternoon. Periodically the children are marched to the next-door church, where they sing hymns, receive the sacraments, recite long prayers, attend devotions to the Virgin Mary, and listen to exhortations by the parish priest. Whatever education takes place in this sectarian environment, these observers feel, is purely incidental to the true purpose of the school. Because many uninformed people have an approximation of this image in the back of their minds, they are—quite understandably—as much opposed

[1] Though the term "parochial" is commonly interchanged with the term "Catholic" in reference to the schools, they do not mean the same thing. A Catholic parochial school is a parish-sponsored school; a Catholic school may be either a parochial school or a private, independent institution.

to any form of government assistance for these schools as they would be to government aid for Catholic churches themselves. The statement, sometimes heard, that the public school educates for citizenship and the religious school educates for sectarian purposes is indicative of this kind of thinking.

The preceding chapters have dwelt at length on the reasons why the American public school in its historical evolution has never been able to provide what Catholics consider a complete education. As we have seen, the original Protestant atmosphere in the public schools has today been largely replaced by either a naturalist humanism or a religious neutralism, neither of which is compatible with the traditional Christian philosophy of education. In the present chapter we propose to discuss this philosophy in which the answers to many questions about the Catholic school, and why it is different, are to be found. A clear understanding of the Catholic philosophy of education should also serve to clarify some of the common misunderstandings about the purpose of a religious school and its place in American society. Non-Catholics are not alone in some of these misapprehensions.

There are Catholic apologists, for example, who explain the rationale of the Catholic school with the simple statement that it exists "to save souls." This is true but misleading. Such a statement requires careful explanation. It would be just as true to say that the purpose of Catholic hospitals, asylums, retreat houses, parishes, foreign missions, or, for that matter, of any church-related undertaking is "to save souls."

Evidently then, the saving of souls is too general an explanation of the school's purpose. It fails to indicate the specific objective, that which distinguishes the school *as such* from the hospital, the asylum, the retreat house, the parish, or the foreign mission. Each of these activities has its own immediate and specifying end or purpose. Since the saving of souls is also the purpose of all these other works, it can be no more than a description of the school's ultimate purpose—a purpose the school necessarily shares in the absolute order with all other human undertakings.

A corollary of the "to-save-souls" explanation of the purpose of the Catholic school is that the school's function is primarily to teach the catechism. Paradoxically, if this were true there would be no need for separate Catholic schools, and there would be no convincing reason why Catholic children should not attend the public schools. One could rightly claim this as the principal task of the school if there were no other way of formally presenting religious doctrine to children save by means of separate schools. But there have always been other ways of supplementing secular education with religious instruction: by classes in the church hall before or after school hours, by parental instruction, by home visits of a special teacher, by instructions at daily Mass, by released-time and dismissed-time programs. Almost any of these substitutes, or a combination, could be a sufficient and certainly less costly method of formally teaching religion. The teaching of the formulas of the Catholic faith, therefore, cannot be either the exclusive or even the primary function of the Catholic school, let alone its reason for existence.

But is it not true, however, that in conducting schools the Catholic Church seeks to make good Catholics and that the priests and Brothers and Sisters who teach in Catholic schools are agents of the Roman Catholic Church? Isn't it evident then that the Catholic school has primarily a sectarian purpose?

This argument confuses the purpose of the work (*finis operis*) with the purpose or *motive* of the worker (*finis operantis*). Failure to distinguish the motivation or reason why an agent engages in an activity from the formality of the activity itself results in the kind of dilemma wherein one is supposedly confronted with the stark choice of the flag or the cross, country or faith—and ultimately, Caesar or God! Are we really compelled to choose between a public school dedicated to producing American citizens and a religious school dedicated to producing Roman Catholics?[2] The traditional Christian philosophy of education sees no antagonism between the two ideals of dedicated citizenry and religious allegiance but conceives them as perfectly compatible and complementary. Why? Because strictly speaking, the primary purpose of the school is neither one. The school *as such* has its own *raison d'être*: it exists primarily—*formally* is the philosophical term—to develop the morally intelligent person. As a member of human society, and depending upon the accidents of time, space,

---

[2] This is simply a variation of the contrived dilemma: Can a practicing Catholic be a loyal American? Is membership in a supernatural society consistent with full membership in a natural society of the political order?

and grace, the same person may simultaneously be a loyal citizen of the American republic and a faithful member of the Catholic Church.

As we shall shortly see, several agencies responsible for education in society make use of the school to attain their appropriate social objectives, but in the process the school does not lose its identity. In other words, the school guards its nature and basic purpose—to produce persons—regardless of the reasons different societies, natural or supernatural, may have in sponsoring educational activity. The state enters into education because it wants these persons as *citizens* to possess the necessary knowledge of their civic duties and privileges, as well as a certain level of physical, intellectual, and moral culture commensurate with the common good. The state's motive does not essentially alter the nature of the school. The Church founds schools so that these persons as her communicants will better acquire the supreme integrating principle of supernatural wisdom in ordering the knowledge, skills, and attitudes they learn. Nor does the Church's motive change the nature of the school.

What has been said regarding the social motives of institutions engaged in education is equally applicable to the motives of teachers. A person may enter teaching for a variety of reasons. He may love to be with young people, or enjoy the school environment, or be ambitious to become a famous teacher, or need the money, or want to follow a family tradition, or be moved by some other consideration. Any one of these motives, or a combination of them, can be the purpose the person has in teaching, but the nature of the teaching process itself does not change with the motive. This holds equally true when a priest or a teaching Sister or Brother enters the classroom of a religious school. He or she may be impelled by one of the considerations just mentioned, but the chief motive, normally, will be to spread Christ's message among men or "to save souls." Nor should this be surprising among persons who have consecrated their lives to laboring for the spiritual good of others.

Nonetheless, a sense of "mission" arising from the commitment to a religious society does not dispense a teacher from his formal duty of teaching, and the same holds true for one's attachment to a political party, a patriotic organization, or a social philosophy.

The teaching process may be modified by the cross-play of other legitimate aims. In the concrete, "teaching activity may be carried out so as to promote virtue and to allow the influence of dedicated personalities full play."[3] Despite their importance, however, this secondary aim must remain incidental and subordinate to the primary activity of teaching.

One of the clearest statements of the purpose and scope of Catholic education was written thirty years ago by Pius XI in his encyclical letter, "The Christian Education of Youth" (*Divini Illius Magistri*). The entire letter repays careful study for its well-balanced explanation of the nature of education, the division of rights in education, the subject and environment of education, and the end and object of Christian education. We have selected here a few central passages of this authoritative statement that will serve as a starting point for a discussion of the theological and philosophical bases of traditional Christian education.[4]

> ITS NATURE. Since education consists essentially in preparing man for what he must be and for what he must do here below, in order to attain the sublime end for which he was created, it is clear that there can be no true education which is not wholly directed to man's last end. . . .[5]
>
> IMPACT OF REVELATION. In the present order of providence, since God has revealed Himself to us in the Person of His Only Begotten Son, who alone is "the way, the truth and the life," there can be no ideally perfect education which is not Christian education.
>
> THE COMMON GOAL. The proper and immediate end of Christian education is to co-operate with divine grace in forming the

[3] Dean Robert J. Henle, S.J., of the St. Louis University Graduate School, has developed this idea in several talks on education.

[4] "Education" is a broader term than "schooling," or that part of education which is the formal responsibility of the school. All of man's capabilities should be developed. This development, however, is not the sole responsibility of the school, for there are other educative agencies in society. The encyclical discusses the work of all these agencies.

[5] In stating that education should be wholly directed to man's last end or, what we have earlier called, the saving of man's soul, we might point out that this, too, is a description of the ultimate and general purpose of all education—formal and informal—and is not a definition of the specifying end of the school as such.

true and perfect Christian, that is, to form Christ Himself in those regenerated by baptism. . . .

THE RESULT. The true Christian, product of Christian education, is the supernatural man who thinks, judges and acts constantly and consistently in accordance with right reason illumined by the supernatural light of the example and teaching of Christ.

BROAD SCOPE. Christian education takes in the whole aggregate of human life, physical and spiritual, intellectual and moral, individual, domestic and social. . . .

SUPERNATURAL PERFECTS THE NATURAL. [Christian education takes in the whole aggregate of human life] not with a view of reducing it in any way, but in order to elevate, regulate and perfect it, in accordance with the example and teaching of Christ.[6]

Some of the fundamental truths stated or implied here by the Pontiff are propositions of the natural order, whose truth man can reason to unaided by revelation, and others are of the supernatural order that have been revealed in the sacred scriptures. Together they form a perennial unchanging charter which, from the beginning of the Christian era, has guided Catholic education and can be called the solid core of its philosophy. These might be briefly set down as follows:

Philosophical Bases

1. There is a personal God whose existence can be proved by reason.

2. Man was put upon earth by God for a purpose in keeping with man's nature.

3. Man is a "person," that is, a rational free being whose perfection consists in knowing and possessing truth, beauty and goodness.

4. Though man's material body gives him a continuity with nature, his spiritual soul indicates a destiny that transcends the purely material and temporal order.

[6] Except for the headings added to each paragraph, these excerpts are taken verbatim from the encyclical. (It has been published in a convenient pamphlet form by the America Press, 70 East 45th St., New York 17, N.Y.)

Theological or Revealed Bases

1. God gave man the added gift of a "supernature" by means of which he would be able to share, after a trial, in the divine life.

2. Adam, the first man, fell from God's favor and, as head of the human race, lost for his descendants the conditionally promised supernatural life.

3. The Eternal Son of God became incarnate to redeem man and to restore him to God's grace and the supernatural life. This restoration takes place by man's incorporation into Christ.

4. Accordingly, the educated Christian is formed in the example and teaching of Christ, the perfect man.

5. The supernatural order does not extinguish nor diminish the values of right reason and the natural order, nor the natural rights of the individual, the home or society itself in what regards education.

The starting point in the Catholic philosophy of education, then, is the reality of the supernatural as revealed through and in Jesus Christ. The Catholic belief that man is a creature of God destined to share in the divine life answers the two questions upon which every philosophy of education is built: What is man? What is his purpose? This sharing in the divine life is actually begun at the moment of baptism, when sanctifying grace and the virtues of faith, hope, and charity—man's supernatural faculties—are infused into the soul. That life, begun on earth through faith, is consummated in a beatific union with God in glory hereafter. For a Catholic this truth is not only the ultimate purpose and final objective of education; it is the theological integrating principle, the philosophical guide, and the basic sanction of the moral order.

Little wonder is it that this uncompromising supernatural bias in Catholic education has always been a scandal and an affront to humanists and secularists. As the late William J. McGucken, S.J., has penetratingly written:

Nothing is more irritating to the modern than this dogma of the supernatural, a dogma that cannot be proved by anthropology, history, psychology or any other human science. Yet nothing is more certain than this, that all traditional historic Christianity is inextricably bound up with it. It cannot be demonstrated by human reason; it requires God's revelation to bring to our knowledge this fact that man is super-naturalized.[7]

The Catholic concept of education situates man against the backdrop of the total society in which he lives and develops. The involved process by which man arrives at adult perfection in society is *education*. Since education is as extensive as human life itself, different agencies in society share rights and responsibilities in this broad field. For man is born into three societies of the large society: the family, civil society (including the state), and the Church. Each has distinct rights, yet all are properly ordered to ensure balance and harmony within the total educational process.

The family into which man is born has the primary right and obligation to educate. This right is prior to the rights of civil and ecclesiastical society because it is based on the natural relation of parents to their offspring, which is the most basic in nature. Common sense, a venerable tradition in Western free society, and several important U. S. Supreme Court decisions would seem to have placed the priority of family right beyond dispute. Unhappily, with the state every year playing an increasing role in education, there are grounds for concern in our own country. There are public school apologists and philosophers of education who simply take it for granted that since public education is under the immediate control of the state it must be both for the sake of the state and primarily a function of the state. It seems necessary from time to time to recall that the U. S. Supreme Court has, on several occasions, unqualifiedly reaffirmed the principle that "the child is not the mere creature of the state" (*Pierce* v. *Society of Sisters*, 1925); and that "the custody, care and nurture of the child reside first in the parents" (*Prince* v. *Massachusetts*, 1944).

Unambiguous support for the primacy of the family right is likewise to be found in the *Universal Declaration of Human Rights*, proclaimed by the General Assembly of the United Nations on December 10, 1948:

---

[7] *The Philosophy of Catholic Education* (America Press pamphlet), p. 12.

Article 16 [3] The family is the natural and fundamental group unit of society and is entitled to protection by society and the state.

Article 26 [3] Parents have a prior right to choose the kind of education that shall be given to their children.

After pointing out how the Church has defended this parental right against the encroachments of the state, Pius XI's encyclical, "The Christian Education of Youth," speaks of the Church's own respect for it: "So jealous is she of the family's inviolable natural right to educate the children that she never consents, save under peculiar circumstances and with special cautions, to baptize the children of infidels, or provide for their education against the will of the parents, till such time as the children can choose for themselves and freely embrace the faith."

However, the family right in education is not an absolute and despotic one, but is, in the words of Pius XI, "dependent on the natural and divine law, and therefore subject alike to the authority and jurisdiction of the Church, and to the vigilance and administrative care of the state in view of the common good." Familial society is not self-sufficient but must achieve its temporal development in civil society in unison with other family units. In this respect, then, in view of the common good of the aggregate of families, civil society has a pre-eminence over the family. We express this pre-eminence when we speak of the *common* welfare as the chief concern of the state, or when we identify the purpose of the state as the securing of the blessings of peace and temporal prosperity for all. In contrast to the family, civil society is self-sufficient or a perfect society of the natural order, as the Church is also a perfect society of the supernatural order. What is meant by the term "perfect" society? This means merely a society which is morally guaranteed (i.e., has the moral right to claim and exercise) all the means necessary to fulfill its direct purposes. In other words, it has sufficient resources within its natural organization and need not go outside itself for assistance to achieve its direct purpose.

When we speak of the Church and civil society as being "perfect" we do not, however, mean that neither has any need of the co-operation of the other. The well-being of every state depends, not immediately and directly, but mediately and indirectly upon the moral integrity of its people. Yet the state, as such, has no adequate means to teach its people a moral code. This is the special function of the Church, which does have adequate means to perform it. Hence the state indirectly depends on the Church to provide it with citizens who respect civil authority, who are virtuous, law-abiding, and ready, whenever necessary, to subordinate selfish interests to the common good.

Likewise the Church, on its side, is independent of the state; but it still has need of the state's assistance for its well-being. As a minimum, the Church depends on the state to maintain an orderly and just social and political environment within which it can carry out its teaching mission.

Before we embark upon a discussion of the mutual rights and proper relationships in education between the two great social institutions of Church and state, it seems almost essential that we first recall certain rock-bottom truths about human society itself, in which Church and state perform basic but distinct functions. Those who refuse to accept these fundamental truths about human society naturally refuse to accept Catholic teaching about the reciprocal relations of Church and state in education. As so often happens, the conflict of opinions over the immediate question is traceable to disagreement about more basic assumptions regarding human nature.

For Church and state, according to the traditional Christian understanding, both form part of God's over-all purpose and plan for the orderly living of human life on this planet. Human life is ordained for certain divine purposes. Some of these purposes are to be attained in time, others only in eternity. A person whose perspectives are limited to this world is not likely to be very sympathetic to the Church in the first place, because the Church is the special institution God has established to lead men to eternal life. Much of the controversy over Church and state springs from the refusal of secularists and the strange failure even of spokesmen for religion to begin where Catholics begin—with a clear statement of the primacy of man's spiritual destiny in the hierarchy of human values. Secularists—and by the term we mean here those who regard man's earthly life as the be-all and end-all of human purposes—look at the life of man upside down.

This disagreement (which is usually assumed, not expressed) about why we are on earth creates an almost unbridgeable gulf between believers and unbelievers when it comes to striking a right balance between the respective jurisdictions of Church and state in education. It is like trying to come to terms with a Christian Scientist on the proper role of the state in promoting public health. If a person assumes that bodily illness is a fiction corresponding to no objective reality, how can anyone not making the same assumption work out (with him) a mutually acceptable set of principles and policies for the promotion of public health?

God created man a "social" being. This truth is clear from observation. It has been recognized and explained by philosophers, from Plato to John Dewey. They mean that the natural, normal, and, in fact, only way in which a human personality can develop is as a member of society, of which the family is the basic unit. This is true because human needs can be satisfied only through a system of social co-operation. An infant needs food, clothing, and shelter. A child and youth requires education and companionship. On a much more complicated scale, an adult needs protection against violence, steady and profitable employment, and an environment in which he can develop his talents, increase his knowledge of God's purposes, and carry into execution the dictates of his conscience. All these and other similar needs require organized co-operation for their fulfillment. Social organization, or what we call "society" (in the most general sense), is therefore a natural exigency of man's nature.

We know that even in relatively simple societies the network of social co-operation becomes quite complicated. If members of society are left without some co-ordinating principle to stabilize the processes of social co-operation (for example, some authority to keep the peace, regulate traffic, water supply, property rights, etc.), society falls a prey to chaos and lawlessness. This, in fact, is what has happened in our day to international society.

Society, therefore, needs an over-all authority to keep the conduct of its members within orderly bounds. This authority, which we call *political*, resides in the state. The state, therefore, is political society acting through the organ of government. The so-called *functions* or kinds of activity belonging to the state all derive from its prime purpose—the protection and promotion of the common good on earth, within the bounds of time. The safeguarding of individual and family rights, of course, forms an important part of the common good. So not only society in general, but its political organization in the form of the state, is also an exigency of human nature.

Whatever functions are assigned to the state, let us notice, they are all—at least the direct functions—*temporal* in purpose, since the direct purpose of the state is confined to its role in time. In eternity there will be no states, their functions having all lapsed with the end of the world.

When we say that the state arises out of human needs, we mean that Almighty God has given His human creatures a nature, a social nature, morally requiring the establishment of political authority. Hence the state arises ultimately through the ordinance of God. The authority it needs to do the work required of it, therefore, ultimately comes from God. That is why the state is called a *natural* society, that is, a society for which God created an inescapable exigency when He created man the kind of being he is. In this wise the state is demanded by what is known as *the natural law*, a shorthand expression for the divine law of morality imbedded in human nature by virtue of the moral needs of man as God made him.

The Church performs quite different functions and had a quite different origin. It did not grow out of a need in man's nature as God created it, but was directly established by Christ to repair the effects of man's fall from the state of grace to which God had elevated it. Hence it did not exist until the time of Christ. God intervened in human history. He revealed supernatural truths about Himself and the supernatural order to which He has elevated mankind. He made belief in these truths necessary to eternal salvation. And He established an infallible authority, a Church, to teach them, to dispense the sacraments conferring His grace and, in general, to guide men toward their heavenly goal.

This great divine intervention in human history, the establishment of the Catholic Church, therefore, created an entirely new need in the proper ordering of man's social and political life. It brought about new relationships in all natural social and political institutions in their confrontation of the supernatural mission of Christ's Church in human society.

So the Church has a purpose quite different from that of the state: to lead men not only to a goal beyond the framework of time but to one inexpressibly more exalted than any natural destiny in eternity. This new goal is nothing less than the face-to-face vision of God forever. The problem of properly relating Church and state is, therefore, that of preserving the God-given rights of both societies while making whatever adjustments are necessary in the natural ordering of human life to co-ordinate it with the supernatural ordering of man's life on earth. This is the Church-state problem in a nutshell.

The problem arises because God did not destroy the natural ordering of human life, but gave it a higher orientation. The natural, being of a lower order, must accordingly respect the primacy of the supernatural.

So even though Church and state are independent and sovereign in their own spheres, these spheres are, as in the spiritual and material aspects of man's own nature, of unequal dignity and importance. The spiritual concerns of man, which, according to religious belief, God has entrusted to His Church, are of a higher order than those concerns entrusted to the state. To keep "first things first" in the order God has created, the entire temporal order, including the state, must be in some wise subordinated to man's eternal destiny. This is what has been traditionally called "the primacy of the spiritual."

Anyone who considers the primacy of the spiritual a sectarian dogma of one church might reflect that this is the religious tradition of the West. The tradition is admirably reflected in this decision of the U. S. Supreme Court:

> The victories for freedom of thought recorded in our Bill of Rights recognize that in the domain of conscience there is a moral power higher than the state. Throughout the ages men have suffered death rather than subordinate their allegiance to God to the authority of the state. Freedom of religion guaranteed by the First Amendment is the product of that struggle (*Girouard* v. *U. S.*, 1946).

Now this primacy of the spiritual is in the sphere of conscience: basically in the individual conscience, but also in the *collective* conscience. Individual men freely adhere to what they believe is a divinely established institution, the Catholic Church, which claims the right, with divine authority, to instruct the consciences of its subjects, whether they are acting as individuals, as parents, as businessmen, as citizens, or as public officials. To the secularist ear this may sound authoritarian and undemocratic—even totalitarian and "un-American." The Catholic simply replies that democracy is not a religion but a form of government, that religion is ultimately God's business and that he believes God has told mankind, both in the Old and New Testaments, in rather detailed fashion, how He is to be worshipped. To many Protestants submission to a church seems an unconscionable restriction on religious freedom. They should strive to understand, however, that Catholics freely accept this limitation as an integral part of their faith. To ask Catholics to "Americanize" or "democratize" their religious faith by modifying the nature of the Church is to ask them to cease to be Catholics.

Those who object to the role the Catholic Church claims for itself by divine right seem to assume that only individual consciences must be respected in American democracy, that when the corporate Catholic conscience speaks upon moral and ethical issues, somehow this is an unwarrantable interference with democratic processes. But this is reductively a sectarian view of religious liberty. Why? Because the religious faith which the individual Catholic holds as necessary to eternal salvation includes *his belief* that the Church has authority to speak out on the morality of public measures, and the belief that the individual Catholic conscience is obliged to respect this authority.

To restrict religious liberty to individuals is, therefore, to impose through the coercive power of the state the classical Protestant view of the nature of spiritual authority, according to which the sole tribunal of moral judgment on this earth is "private judgment." Again, this view, in effect, denies to a Catholic the right to be a Catholic, to hold the *Catholic* religion. You may be a Catholic, it says, but you must change the nature of your church. This is as unfair as to tell someone: "You may continue to be a Jew, but you may not follow the dietary habits that symbolize your religious dedication." This Catholic belief does, it is true, endow Catholics with a much greater coherence in society than that provided for by the more atomistic religious philosophy of Protestantism. But this hardly is a valid reason for challenging the propriety of the Catholic system as "un-American."

The status of a child as a member of a family, as we have seen, takes priority over his status as a citizen of the state. At the same time, however, the state has certain rights in the field of education, flowing from its purpose. The Catholic understanding of "the true and just rights of the state in the education of its citizens" has been clearly stated in Pope Pius XI's encyclical. The state has a right, even a duty, to make sure that its young citizens acquire such "civic education" as they need in order to help promote "the common welfare in the temporal order." To this end, declared the Holy Father,

> . . . the state can exact, and take measures to secure, that all its citizens have the necessary knowledge of their civic and political duties, and a certain degree of physical, intellectual and moral culture, which, considering the conditions of our times, is really necessary for the common good.[8]

The state is acting within its right when it requires that children possess basic knowledge and skills so that they may not become a burden to the community or fall short of the standard of good citizenship. Thus, it is entirely appropriate for the state to require courses in history and government so that its youthful citizens will come to understand and love the traditions of the nation and will be prepared to discharge the duties of citizenship.

Moreover, the state has an obligation to protect and foster the prior rights of the family in the process of education. The parental right is given for the sake of the child. Therefore, the state is bound to protect the right of the child itself, when the parents are incompetent, negligent, or delinquent. The state promotes education by encouraging and assisting the initiative and activity of the family.[9] The complexity of modern living has made it all but

[8] Ibid., p. 15.
[9] Between 1891 and 1893 a lively controversy took place among Catholic educators over the nature and extent of the state's right to educate. It was precipitated by a pamphlet, *Education, to Whom Does It Belong?*, in which

impossible for a single family to provide within the home an adequate formal education for its children. When the state steps in and mobilizes the resources of the whole community to make up what is wanting in the resources of its members as individuals and family groups, it is assisting the parents, not taking over from them. In providing the means of formal schooling the state is supplying for and co-operating with the parent, not replacing him. As we shall see in a succeeding chapter, the American state-supported system of education has been built up without full consideration of this principle. The rights of the state in education, it can hardly be repeated too often, are secondary and derived from parental delegation. Once again, support for this principle can readily be found in our legal history.

Control over the education of their children belongs primarily to parents, since those who bring children into this world must assume the primary responsibility for their proper rearing and schooling. The duty of parents certainly includes seeing that their children receive proper instruction for both their temporal and spiritual destinies. No matter how radically philosophies of education differ, every one of them agrees that education includes formation or the inculcation of values. Education of the young is for Catholics, particularly a spiritual and religious concern.

Catholics believe that education, as a basically ethical undertaking, is necessarily connected with man's supernatural goal. Since the Church was established by Christ to guide men to that goal, education becomes a proper function of the Church. By making His Church the gateway to eternal life, God has endowed His religious society with essential rights over the education of the baptized. God set up His Church precisely to provide, largely through religious instruction and training, the means to learn the supernatural truths He has revealed and the practices of the Christian religion He has made obligatory.

---

the author, Rev. Thomas Bouquillon, argued that the state had a special and proper right to teach human knowledge. The majority of Catholic educators of that period insisted that, since the state's right was only substitutional, arising from the default of parents, it was limited to the minimum necessary for the preservation of the state. Father Bouquillon defended compulsory education laws—still widely unpopular at the time—but denied the need or propriety of a compulsory state school system. See D. F. Reilly, *The School Controversy* (Washington: Catholic Univ. Press, 1943).

The Catholic Church, therefore, possesses the pre-eminent right in education—pre-eminent precisely because of the primacy of the supernatural order. The Church holds that her right to teach is a power vested in her directly by her Divine Founder Himself. She is not, therefore, like other voluntary associations in society dependent upon the civil power for the privilege of teaching. "She cannot admit, therefore, that any earthly power can deprive her of her right to teach. That right inheres in her very nature as an autonomous society, one whose constitution is altogether independent of the state. If the Church were not allowed to teach she would be bereft of one of her basic functions; she would be condemned, as under Communist totalitarianism today, to a twilight existence and, by every human augury, to gradual extinction."[10]

Parents who recognize the divine authority of the Church are therefore obliged to follow its teachings and regulations regarding the education of their children.

In ideal, all these rights—those of parent, Church, and state—work in harmony for the benefit of the individual. The supernatural order, to which the Church owes her rights, does not annihilate the natural order, to which pertain the rights of parent and state, but completes and elevates it. The reason for this harmony, as Pope Pius said, "is because both come from God, who cannot contradict Himself: 'The works of God are perfect and all His ways are judgements.'"

What are the principal benefits that a Catholic parent and pastor find in a Catholic education? They can be grouped around these four points.

1. The child learns systematically and thoroughly about his religion. He obtains a formal knowledge of the truths of Christian revelation, including the existence and nature of God, Christ's Incarnation and Redemption, Christ's Church and the workings of the Holy Spirit within it, the history of the chosen people and of the Church.

2. He enjoys regular opportunities, direct and indirect, for

[10] "The Teaching Mission of the Church," annual statement of the American hierarchy, November 15, 1958. Reprinted in *The Catholic Mind*, March–April 1959.

the deepening of his sense of religious dedication. He has ready access to the Mass and the sacraments; he learns to live a fuller life of prayer; he acquires a practical knowledge and love of the Church's liturgical life.

3. The child learns an ordering of knowledge in an atmosphere in which the spiritual and the supernatural hold the primacy in the hierarchy of temporal and eternal values. He learns that his faith is not something apart but is related to the whole texture of life.

4. He acquires a "Catholic" attitude or outlook on life based upon the firm knowledge of his duties and privileges as a follower of Christ; he gains pride and love—and loyalty to—his Catholic heritage.

These four categories cannot, however, be treated as if they were independent of one another. They are closely related, for each is an aspect of Christian growth, each fuses with and reinforces the others. The result is Christian education in all its dimensions—than which no loftier or more perfect educational ideal has ever been conceived.[11]

Knowledge is not faith, but since faith is an intellectual virtue, the two go hand in hand. Acquaintance with the object of belief and an awareness of one's motives for belief are the ordinary prerequisites for firm assent. So systematized instruction has importance here. A person learns religion in somewhat the same way he learns a language. If he is fortunate enough to be raised in the country where the tongue is spoken, he will almost always have a far better grasp of the language than he would through intense self-instruction or private tutoring or enrollment in a special class. It is axiomatic that residence in a country facilitates the acquisition of a second language. Here is the learner's great advantage, when instruction in the Catholic faith takes place within a Catholic school. He not only gets a more complete and systematic instruction in the formal truths of his religion, but he is "in the new country" and the atmosphere reinforces and hastens the process of learning.

[11] It hardly needs saying that the school by itself cannot achieve this ideal of Catholic education. The work of the school must be built on what the home has already done and continues to do.

Despite the fact that religion is taught formally for only brief periods, its influence pervades other areas of the curriculum. Religious themes receive proportionate treatment in other courses where they are integral to the subject. This will occur particularly in literature, history, and social studies. A student receives and organizes new knowledge according to his previous disposition. If he is convinced that man is only the accidental outcome of 10,000 millennia of nature's fluid evolutionary process, his receptivity will differ markedly from that of a Christian believer. Faith is never departmental: all things fall within its purview. This suggestion of the late Pius XII, made in a talk to a group of teachers in 1957, illustrates the point:

> When you study nature, remember that "it was through Him that all things came into being, and without Him came nothing that has come to be" (John 1:3). When you study history, remember that it is not a simple enumeration of more or less bloody or edifying facts, because one can easily detect a pattern which becomes a subject of profound study in the light of universal Divine Providence and the unquestionable human freedom of action. Note especially how you would look upon the events of the past 2,000 years with other eyes, if you would consider them as the development of Christian civilization, starting with those events which marked the dawn of the Church, dwelling upon the great unsurpassed syntheses made in ancient times and during the Middle Ages, reflecting upon the distressful apostasies but also the great modern discoveries and looking with confidence at the signs of rebirth and recovery.

The encyclical on "The Christian Education of Youth" speaks of the educational environment of the Church as embracing "the sacraments, divinely efficacious means of grace, the sacred ritual, so wonderfully instructive and the material fabric of her churches, whose liturgy and art have an immense educational value." This brings in the parish. A thorough religious education can result only from the joint effort of all agencies concerned with the child's formation—home, school, and parish. Hence the liturgical life of the Church into which the child is initiated is lived not only in the parish church but in the school and the home as well. The parochial school is deliberately situated near the parish church, and this proximity makes for close co-operation in religious education and formation. If a school is distant from the church, it probably has its own chapel.

Each year the liturgical cycle of the Church recounts the story of God's two great interventions in time: creation and salvation. But the liturgical cycle is more than the re-enactment of history. God's dialogue with mankind continues in the Mass and the sacraments. As one writer has put it, "By taking part in the life of the liturgy and by following the cycle of the Church year, the Christian enters into the vast stream of grace set in motion by God since the foundation of the world. Thus an historical catechesis is made complete only by a liturgical catechesis."[12] Prayer and religious devotion are a natural growth of parochial school life. Group participation in liturgical practices and sacramental rites, when they are part of the school routine, gives them complete normalcy and acceptability. These observances fit easily into the school day and follow a natural rhythm in the school calendar.

The Mass and the reception of the sacraments are central to the devotional life of a Catholic. Accordingly, the Catholic child is carefully instructed during the first two grades of elementary school to prepare him for his first confession and communion. The beautiful ceremony of the First Communion traditionally occurs at a parish Mass on Mother's Day or on some other Sunday in spring. When the children are older and have been more fully instructed in the faith, they are qualified to receive the sacrament of confirmation from the bishop. This occasion, too, is an important milestone in the life of the young Christian.

Pupils are encouraged to attend the daily Mass in the parish church before the opening of the school day, especially on important feast days and during the liturgical seasons of Lent and Advent. Some schools require daily Mass attendance. Others prescribe Mass on one day of the week, but most schools leave the children free in this matter at all times. A few schools begin the regular school day with Mass as the opening period, a practice borrowed from some European countries. In many parishes the

[12] "General Tendencies in Contemporary Catechetics," Pierre Ranwez, S.J., in *Shaping the Christian Message*, ed. Gerard S. Sloyan (New York: Macmillan, 1958), p. 118.

school children attend their own Sunday Mass, at which a special instruction or sermon is given. On one school day of each month the children are allowed a special period to visit the church to receive the sacrament of confession or, if they prefer, merely to enter the confessional to ask for the priest's blessing.

During his parochial school days a Catholic youngster is closer to the liturgy than at any other period in his life. From September to June he acquires a familiarity in his daily living with the saints and seasons of the Church. Along with the heroes of his country's history, the youngster gets acquainted with the great men and women of the Church world. He observes the season of Advent in preparation for the Birthday of Christ, Christmas, and the season of Lent in preparation for the Resurrection of Christ, Easter. The boys learn to assist at Mass and other liturgical functions, while the girls—often the boys too—learn to sing the sacred chants and choral music that accompany these ceremonies. These activities, however, when they are not extracurricular, are confined to the period regularly assigned for religion study or music study. Seasonal classroom decorations are other reminders of the liturgical year; for example, that November is dedicated to the Suffering Souls in Purgatory, that May is dedicated to the Blessed Virgin Mary. The classroom bulletin boards and displays tell in picture and poster about the missionary work of the Church at home and abroad, of the creation of new cardinals or the canonization of a new saint.

Probably the most distinctive, certainly the most important, benefit of education within a Catholic school is the ordering of knowledge in an atmosphere wherein the spiritual and the supernatural are properly ordered in the hierarchy of values. The Catholic philosophy of education is based on the reality of the supernatural and its primacy in the total scheme of things. The values, goals, and ideals of the natural order—important and worthy of pursuit as these may be—are subordinate in Catholic eyes to those of the supernatural order. For in reality the order created by God was never a purely natural order, but from its inception was elevated to the supernatural. The lapse of Adam from grace did not destroy this fundamental ordering; it did result in an antagonism between the material and spiritual orders, particularly within man himself.

Nor is the Fall of man one of those sectarian items which can be dismissed as not really relevant to the large questions in education. William J. McGucken has called attention to the fact that two modern philosophers, Friedrich Foerster, a devout Lutheran, and Bertrand Russell, the modern skeptic, both have arrived independently at the same conclusion: that in the last analysis all theories of education are dependent on the views taken of the dogma of original sin. For all theories hinge on the nature of the person to be educated. Calvinism and Lutheranism held that, in consequence of the Fall, human nature was depraved; Catholicism teaches that human nature was deprived of the supernatural life; Rousseau and Dewey attempted to dismiss the whole notion.

The Catholic school shares with the home and Church the responsibility of teaching the child that "his chief significance comes from the fact that he is created by God and is destined for life with God in eternity." In order to live in a modern society where "social, moral, intellectual and spiritual values are everywhere disintegrating," the child needs the integrating force of religion— a force that will arm him with a complete and rational meaning for his existence.

The Catholic bishops of the United States in their annual statement for 1950 described in detail the effects of this religious force:

> First of all, it will arouse in him a consciousness of God and of eternity. His vision will be opened out upon a supernatural world revealed by faith which differs from the world of nature his senses reveal.
>
> Secondly, it will give him a continuing purpose in life, for it will teach him that he was made to know, love and serve God in this world as the condition for meriting eternal happiness.
>
> Thirdly, it will induce in him a deep sense of responsibility for those rights and obligations he possesses by reason of his citizenship in heaven as well as on earth.
>
> Finally, religion will challenge him to sanctify whatever walk of life he chooses and to seek and accept the Will of God in whatever way it may be manifested.

Thus, as a principle of integration, religion will help the child to develop *a sense of God, a sense of direction, a sense of responsibility,* and *a sense of mission* in this life.

These principles are not taught day by day by means of blackboard diagrams and class recitations. In a gentle imperceptible manner, however, their meaning is absorbed and they become quietly operative in the life of the Catholic child. Certain traditional religious symbols silently telling of God, the Incarnation of His Son, man's Redemption by Christ, and the life of the blessed in heaven help to establish this atmosphere of the supernatural. The cross above the school building, the crucifix hanging in every classroom, and other religious symbols that adorn the walls serve constantly to remind the pupils of things that transcend this world. Even the clerical garb of the priest and the religious robes of the Sisters and Brothers—symbolizing dedication to the loftiest values of the spirit—contribute to this effect.

The function of the Catholic school is not merely to teach the formulas of the Catholic religion but, as Father George Bull of Fordham University once said, "to impart in a thousand ways, which defy formularization, the Catholic attitude toward life as a whole." It is Catholicism as a culture, not as a conflicting creed, which is at odds with the spirit of the modern world and in a sense makes Catholics a people apart. A Catholic's belief implicitly affects his whole life, and in many areas of life this puts him at odds with accepted conduct. A culture is not what Ortega y Gasset has called "some sort of ornamental accessory for the life of leisure." Rather, as the same modern philosopher has said:

> Culture is an indispensable element of life, a dimension of our existence, as much a part of man as his hands. True, there is such a thing as man without hands; but that is no longer simply man: it is man crippled. The same is to be said of life without culture, only in a much more fundamental sense. It is life crippled, wrecked, false.[13]

Christian or Christ-centered culture is the supreme integrating principle from which proceeds all activity within a Catholic

[13] José Ortega y Gasset, *Mission of the University* (Princeton Univ. Press, 1944), p. 67.

school. Justice Robert H. Jackson of the U. S. Supreme Court inadvertently gave the reason that above all justifies the existence of a separate Catholic school, when he wrote in his dissent in the *Everson* case: "Our public school, if not a product of Protestantism, at least is more consistent with it than with the Catholic culture and scheme of values."

The Catholic community agrees.

CHAPTER 5

The Catholic School in Operation

Catholic grade school and high school education in America has outgrown its adolescent stage. Childhood is past, but the growing pains, self-consciousness, and occasional misunderstanding remain to dog what Chicago's superintendent of Catholic schools, Monsignor William E. McManus, has called "a bright if uncertain future." The brightness and the uncertainty, we might add, are qualities Catholic education shares with American education in general. For overcrowded classrooms, teacher recruitment and preparation, curriculum standards, gifted and exceptional students, and an inflation-swollen annual budget are all items that bring wrinkles to the brow of Catholic as well as public school leaders. What kind of educational structure has been reared upon the theological and philosophical bases examined in the preceding chapter? What *is* the Catholic school in operation and how does it run?

We can most simply define a Catholic school—whether operated by a parish, a diocese, or a private religious corporation—as an elementary or secondary school that has been canonically authorized and recognized by the bishop in his particular diocese or area of ecclesiastical jurisdiction. In the 140 dioceses of the fifty states there are 16,185 parishes with resident pastors, and nearly 10,000 of these parishes conduct a parochial elementary school. Each parish, like the local school district in the public school system, bears the responsibility for building and operating its own school. A diocesan superintendent appointed by the bishop has general supervision over all parochial schools, but the local pastor functions as the agent for the diocese in managing his own school.

The pastor engages the faculty, collects parish funds for operational expenses, supervises maintenance, plans expansion, and supplies moral support. He does not, however, enter directly into the academic administration, though by reason of his pastoral title he is the head of the school.

The hundreds of teaching sisterhoods have traditionally furnished the faculties of the American parochial schools.[1] To a lesser extent the teaching brotherhoods have been found in the schools, and in recent years the number of priests assigned to teaching has grown measurably. The religious superior of the teaching order generally directs the operation of the school in the dual capacity of principal and superior. Higher superiors in the order make the assignments of superiors, principals, and teachers for the parish and diocesan schools with whom the order has teaching contracts.

In so far as these schools serve indiscriminately all Catholic children of an area, they form the equivalent of a second public school system on the primary school level. These schools enroll about one half of the Catholic population of primary school age. In addition to the strictly parochial institutions there are 407 private and 200 institutional elementary schools, most of which have boarding facilities, with an enrollment of 92,933. The total Catholic elementary school enrollment during 1958–59 was 4,101,-792.[2]

During the decades when our larger American cities all contained immigrant neighborhoods, the ethnic character of these neighborhoods was mirrored in the parochial schools. Predominantly German, Polish, or Irish districts in these cities often gave rise to "national" parishes and parochial schools of German, Polish, or Irish coloring. Such parishes and such schools today, how-

---

[1] Detailed information may be found in *Guide to the Catholic Sisterhoods in the United States*, compiled by Thomas P. McCarthy, C.S.V. (Washington: Catholic Univ. Press, 1958), and in *Official Guide to Catholic Educational Institutions in the United States* (Publishers' Parish Service, 180 Varick St., New York 14, N.Y.).

[2] These statistics were made available to the author through the kindness of the Education Department, National Catholic Welfare Conference, and Rev. John J. Green, O.S.F.S., Associate Secretary for Secondary Schools, National Catholic Educational Association. Because they are based on direct institutional reporting, they are the most reliable figures available.

ever, are a thing of the past, or, where they may still chance to exist, they are rare exceptions.

Until the second decade of the present century secondary school education in the United States generally followed the traditional European pattern, in that the secondary school served as collegiate preparation for the college-bound minority. It is true that ever since the close of the Civil War, the American high school curriculum was being broadened to include a wide range of subjects, but this change simply reflected the broadening of the college curriculum itself. Modern academic subjects—for example, modern languages and science studies—were offered in the secondary school along with the traditional ones, so that the curriculum of the average high school still remained pretty much college preparatory. These curricular offerings were considered the finest instruments for educating students—all students, whether they terminated formal schooling upon graduation from high school or planned to continue on to college.

In 1900 approximately 10 per cent of the total population of high school age was attending secondary schools, and three out of four high school graduates went on to college. In 1957, 88.2 per cent of high school-age youngsters was in high school, and a little over one half of a high school graduating class continued on to college. The contrasting proportions and percentages here are startling evidence of the revolution that has transformed the American high school. Catholic secondary schools have undergone the same change, so that they now are designed to accommodate both terminal and college-bound students.

Back in 1900, however, Catholic secondary schools for boys were practically all preparatory departments of Catholic colleges, and schools for girls were mainly academies under the direction of women's religious communities. The same social demands that widened the scope of public secondary education brought about basic changes in the idea of Catholic secondary schooling. A report of the High School Committee of the Catholic Educational Association at the national meeting of 1911 strongly urged that the parochial and diocesan school programs be expanded to include secondary education. How effectively this recommendation was followed out can be gathered from the fact that today there are

1,566 secondary schools (1958–59 enrollment: 500,304) owned and operated by either parochial or diocesan authorities, in comparison with the 783 private high schools (1958–59 enrollment: 310,464) whose ownership and operation is in the hands of religious communities. The total Catholic secondary school enrollment during 1958–59 was 810,768.[3]

The provision by the public schools for pupils requiring technical and terminal programs of study is to be found more and more in the Catholic high schools, though on a less elaborate and less diversified scale. In 1947, in a survey sponsored by the National Catholic Educational Association 1,581 Catholic high schools identified themselves according to these categories:[4]

Comprehensive	64.4 %
Academic	31.6
Commercial	3.8
Vocational	0.2

The high percentage of strictly academic, i.e., college preparatory, schools is accounted for by the fact that most of the Catholic private schools have remained academically selective in the older tradition. The great expansion of Catholic secondary education in the past twenty years, however, has been largely due to the rise of the central Catholic high school. This is a large (500–1,000 average enrollment) comprehensive-type school operated by the diocese. The parishes served by these central schools are taxed by the diocese for their erection and operation. In 1925 there were sixty-one schools of this type in existence, but in 1958–59 their number had risen to over four hundred. There is every reason to believe that the central Catholic high school under diocesan control will continue to be the main factor in the growth of Catholic secondary education. The total number of Catholic high schools with a less-than-100-pupil enrollment has dwindled to 462. It is interesting to note that this centralizing movement is running parallel to the trend in public school education to consolidate

---

[3] The number of institutions was supplied by N.C.W.C.'s Education Department. The enrollment figures here are from *The Official Catholic Directory for 1959*, and include students in protective institutions.

[4] Sister Mary Janet, *Catholic Secondary Education* (Washington: N.C.W.C., 1949), p. 37.

smaller school districts. The objective in both cases is to provide a more efficient base for the secondary school program.

From earliest times, the conduct of Catholic education in the United States has fallen almost exclusively to the clergy and the religious orders. These teachers are bearers of a rich tradition in the history of education. They are the heirs of the monastic teachers and clerics of the old cathedral schools. They carry on the educational work of John Baptist de la Salle and the Brothers of the Christian Schools, the Brethren of the Common Life, the Jesuits, and other religious teaching groups that helped to make a modern Europe and brought Western learning to many parts of the New World. The nearly 100,000 teaching Sisters in America today have sprung from the great families of religious congregations established in this country during the pioneer decades of the Church.

Through his or her permanent dedication by religious vows a member of a teaching congregation initially has two great advantages as a teacher—vocation and permanency. The demanding labor of teaching can never be adequately compensated for in purely material terms. Consequently, the teacher has always had to be possessed of a sense of vocation and to find his real reward in a love for the world of learning and an eagerness to share the things of the spirit with the youthful mind. In the dedicated celibate life of a Sister or Brother there is no preoccupation with promotion, salary, retirement, and other material benefits which necessarily must occupy the attention of the majority of lay teachers. A married teacher must combine with a teaching career the demanding life of parent and spouse. It is entirely understandable that 42 per cent of the public school teachers have had less than ten years' teaching experience.[5] A life dedicated to teaching the young allows the bulk of the religious teachers to amass a reservoir of experience in teaching that qualifies one truly for the designation of master or doctor of the education process—in the root meaning of these much overworked titles.

At one time there was a basis for the criticism that many religious women teachers began their classroom careers without the

[5] "The Status of the American Public-School Teacher," National Education Association *Research Bulletin*, XXXV, No. 1 (February 1957).

equivalent collegiate and professional training had by their counterparts in the public schools. It was true that many congregations of Sisters followed the practice of sending teachers into the classroom with only two years of concentrated preparation. These young teachers then completed work for the college degree and took additional professional courses during subsequent summer schools.

There was always some warrant for this procedure. (A few decades ago this was common practice for teachers going into public schools too.) The fact that the neophyte teacher lives in a convent community of veteran teachers, and is able therefore to profit from close, friendly supervision and counseling was viewed as a more than adequate compensation for the delay in taking extra courses in formal pedagogy. Moreover, candidates for the teaching sisterhoods are carefully screened to try to ensure that only the well-balanced, talented personality—the type at the top of any teacher-rating scale—steps into a parochial school classroom. Ordinarily this is the kind of person that becomes after a few years of classroom experience a better-than-average teacher.

Catholic educational leadership, however, even before the post-Sputnik stress on stricter academic standards, had insisted on improved professional preparation for parochial school teachers. The reform movement received powerful impetus through the establishment in 1953 of the National Sister Formation Conference. The ideal set by the conference, already realized by many congregations of teaching Sisters, goes beyond the ordinary standards of pre-service and in-service preparation expected of the modern teacher.

The idea of the Sister Formation Conference is, as one leader has expressed it, "that Sisters doing active works in our own times need a long and careful spiritual formation, a general intellectual training which will equip them for a rich personal life and an effective social leadership, and a precise professional preparation which will make them the equals or superiors of lay people doing the same kind of work."[6]

There is every expectation that these new policies for improved

[6] Sister Mary Emil, I.H.M., executive secretary, Sister Formation Conferences, in *America*, January 12, 1957. Three volumes have been published by the Fordham University Press, in which may be found the annual pro-

faculty preparation, when more widely adopted, will further en-
hance the traditional excellence of parochial school education by
bringing weaker systems up to the standards of the best.

The mind of the Church is uncompromisingly clear on this ideal.
"Many of your schools are being described and praised to us as
being very good," the late Pope Pius XII said in an address on
September 15, 1951, to the First International Congress of Teaching Sisters. He expressed his "fervent wish" that all Catholic
schools endeavor to become excellent. That this wish was not a
pious velleity is plain from the Pope's next words, in which he
placed his finger on the chief source of excellence:

> This presupposes that your teaching Sisters are masters of the
> subjects they expound. See to it, therefore, that they are well
> trained and that their education corresponds in quality and
> academic degrees to that demanded by the state. Be generous
> in giving them all they need, especially where books are con-
> cerned, so that they may continue their studies and thus offer
> young people a rich and solid harvest of knowledge. This is in
> keeping with the Catholic idea, which gratefully welcomes all
> that is naturally good, beautiful and true, because it is an image
> of the divine goodness and beauty and truth.

The Supreme Pontiff emphasized the duty of excellence with his
audience of Sisters, the heads of their respective teaching congregations, saying:

> Many parents entrust their daughters to you because their con-
> sciences bid them do so. But this does not mean that the children
> should suffer by receiving in your schools an education of in-
> ferior value. On the contrary, you must do all you can to assure
> parents that their children are getting the best education right
> from the elementary classes.[7]

---

ceedings and studies of the movement. They are *Mind of the Church in the
Formation of Sisters, Spiritual and Intellectual Elements in the Formation of
Sisters,* and *Planning for the Formation of Sisters.*

[7] The Third Plenary Council of Baltimore also held up as an ideal the
perfecting of Catholic schools, and flatly repudiated the notion ". . . that
the Catholic school need be in any respect inferior to any other school what-
soever." Again, the Council said: "And if hitherto, in some places, our people
have acted on the principle that it is better to have an imperfect Catholic
school than to have none, let them now push their praise-worthy ambition

The planning and foundation of schools, the recruiting of the teaching staff, the adoption and implementing of policies, the administration of the schools themselves have been the acknowledged tasks of the diocese or the parish or the religious order. This has been especially true of institutions on the primary and secondary level. Though from the beginning laymen and laywomen have taught in Catholic schools, their role has, until fairly recent times, been completely subordinate.

Lay persons rarely had a voice in the formulation of policies, seldom exercised administrative responsibilities, and were commonly regarded as substitutes for religious teachers, to be replaced when these became sufficiently numerous. The professional status of Catholic lay teachers, with few exceptions, suffered in comparison with that of teachers in other type schools. The lay teacher had to be possessed of a deeper sense of vocation than his counterpart in the public schools, for, like the Sisters and Brothers and priests, he, too, had to fill out his modest recompense in the currency of the intangible. The parish or diocese, again with rare exceptions, simply could not match the salary scale or offer the professional benefits that eventually became standard in the public schools.

A noiseless revolution has been under way for some years in the faculty structure of the Catholic schools. Today, Catholic schools, including the colleges, employ close to 45,000 lay teachers —a ratio of one lay teacher to every three religious or priests, and the proportion has risen dramatically since the close of World War II. Between 1946 and 1959 in the grade schools, 2,768 lay teachers became 22,051—an increase of nearly 800 per cent. In 1959, along with these lay teachers there were 75,914 religious and priests. During the same period the number of high school lay teachers nearly tripled, going from 3,752 to 9,055. There are also 30,422 religious and priests engaged in high school teaching.

If the proportion of the total Catholic school population remains constant, it is predicted that by 1971 there will be more lay teachers than Sisters in the parochial school system. This prediction is based on the present number of preschool children, plus the anticipated number of births in the next few years, the rate of

---

still further, and not relax their efforts till their schools be elevated to the highest educational excellence." (See Guilday, 247.)

Sister vocations, and the rate of increase in lay teachers. During the school year 1958–59 there were approximately 96,819 Sister teachers and 34,411 lay teachers. In 1971 there will be an estimated 121,000 Sister teachers and 137,000 lay teachers.[8]

The day is over, then, when the lay teacher has to feel out of place in the school under clerical or religious direction. Obviously school population pressures have had a great deal to do with altering the old pattern, but new attitudes in the Catholic community would have brought about the change regardless. The old notion of the lay teacher as merely a substitute for a religious teacher is dying out and is yielding to the recognition that the lay teacher holds the key place in any future expansion of Catholic education.

The size of the army of little people whose feet are already pointed toward the doors of the Catholic schools is already known. The number of teachers required to care for these pupils of the 1960s is also known. But where will they come from? Certainly not from the seminaries and novitiates, as a glance at the rate of increase for religious and priestly vocations makes plain. The teaching orders have been blessed with a normal number of vocations but have not met, nor will they have enough subjects to meet, the demands for teachers. The enrollment in Catholic elementary schools alone is growing almost four times as fast as the number of teaching Sisters who thus far have been the mainstay of the parochial school systems. Between 1946 and 1956 the number of religious teachers went up by 22.5 per cent, but the number of lay teachers jumped by 156 per cent.

The Most Reverend Vincent S. Waters, Bishop of Raleigh, speaking of a period many years in the future, made this prophecy:

> The growth of the parochial school system will be so great that Sisters will be supervisors only, of laymen, or of Third Order or Secular Institute member-teachers. Sisters will be largely restricted to the teaching of religion.[9]

---

[8] See the excellent study of this problem by Sister Rose Matthew, I.H.M., "Sister Teachers in the United States: a Study of Their Status and Projected Role," in *Planning for the Formation of Sisters* (New York: Fordham Univ. Press, 1958).

[9] Ibid., p. 61.

Far from deploring these changes, Catholics can look upon them as healthy signs of the coming of age of Catholic education in America. Qualified religious and priests will, please God, always be available in sufficient numbers to give a solid religious spirit to our schools. It need hardly be stated, though, that dedicated personalities, academic preparation, classroom competence, even religious influence itself, can be as much the possession of lay teachers as of religious teachers. There are Catholic parents (and students, too) who, failing to understand this, still regard the lay teacher with a slightly jaundiced eye, as if somehow a "mere" lay person like themselves could not exemplify the loftiest ideals of the Catholic faith. This strange attitude will die out when the lay teacher is accorded full professional recognition and respected as an integral member of the faculty by all those connected with the parish and school.

One can expect that the purely administrative and academic functions of the American Catholic school will more and more become the normal responsibility of the laity, as is already the case in parts of Canada and in many European countries. It has not been a lack of good will but a tradition of isolationism and the general poverty of the Catholic community that has retarded the clerical-lay partnership in Catholic education. For a long time most Catholics believed a Catholic education was something that could be given only by someone wearing a cassock or a Roman collar; the clergy, too, largely shared this belief. Whatever material resources the young Church could tap during the post-Civil War decades of miraculous expansion went into the erection of church buildings and schools. The little money left over scarcely supported the modest living requirements of the religious teachers, and left next to nothing with which to attract lay teachers. The problem of lay salaries has by no means been solved, and it remains today to worry Catholic educational leadership. Many dioceses have taken heroic measures to provide a salary scale and pension benefits that approximate those offered by the public schools of the area. Other dioceses have yet to make a start in this direction. There is no dearth of qualified lay candidates for teaching positions in parish and diocesan schools, when the material compensation even comes close to what competing systems offer. Most lay teachers find the atmosphere, discipline, and standards of the average Catholic school conducive to the happy and successful teaching that is itself a satisfying reward.

Some of the current burdens borne by the parochial school are being eased by the co-operation of laymen, individually and in groups. Mothers' clubs everywhere have long staffed school lunchrooms and cafeterias, but in some dioceses mothers with teaching experience and credentials are now joining the regular school faculties, either as classroom assistants or as full teachers. In many parishes car pools among fathers are a substitute for nonexistent buses. Intramural and extramural athletic programs have expanded, thanks to the assistance furnished the schools by college students. In fact, many of the time-consuming tasks around a school, which formerly were assigned to one of the parish priests, are coming into the hands of qualified lay folk, leaving the priests freer for religious instruction classes and home visits.

The lay activities here described are helping to end the passive, "nonvoting" role, too long the lot of the laity in Catholic education. Catholic laymen and laywomen are taking new pride in *their* schools. A by-product of the increased lay presence in the parochial school has been a lessening of the mistrust the sectarian nature of these institutions once inspired in the community.

Since 1940, under the impact of the baby boom, public school enrollment has shot up 36 per cent, but the enrollment in parochial and other nonpublic schools by 118 per cent. In certain expanding metropolitan and suburban areas, the importuning of parents has meant some Catholic school classes of seventy, eighty, or even ninety children in the lower grades. To avoid this kind of overcrowding many parochial schools operate on double sessions or use prefab portable classrooms and even church basements. Few pastors or parochial school administrators are happy about either overcrowding or basement classrooms.

Before censoring them one might reflect upon the pressures involved and the responsibilities at stake. Catholic parents *want* their youngsters in parochial schools and fight to get them in. Any pastor can tell of cases where young parents have turned down job promotions and declined chances to improve housing or move to better neighborhoods in order to remain near a Catholic school. In spite of an estimated $2 billion put into parochial school con-

struction since the end of World War II, there are still hundreds
of thousands of Catholic youngsters who must be turned away
from parochial schools every fall because of lack of space and
inability to put up new schools fast enough. Recently it was announced in one New York suburban community that there were
a hundred places available for the first-grade class on a first-come,
first-served basis. The night before the spring preschool registration, some one hundred parents formed a line on the sidewalk
in front of the parish school, determined to maintain vigil throughout the night in order to secure a desk for their child. Those parents who came for the registration in the morning were too late:
the quota was filled.[10] Similar cases have been reported in other
sections of the country.

The current shortage of classrooms and teachers in some places
has forced wide consideration of one truly drastic measure: the
elimination of the first four grades of the parochial school. Some
Catholic educators are convinced that, since all children cannot
possibly be accommodated in all twelve grades of elementary and
secondary schooling, present facilities should be used—at least for
the duration of the current crisis—to provide for pupils in the upper grades and in high school. The assumption here is that pre-
adolescent and adolescent boys and girls, i.e., those between ten
and eighteen years of age, have the greatest need of the spiritual
formation and moral discipline of the Catholic school. (Less than
one quarter of the high-school-age group is presently touched by
Catholic schooling.) Advocates of this plan argue that the parish
can establish in the parochial school itself an after-class program
of religious instruction and activities, to which the youngest children could come daily or thrice weekly. During the first two years
the child would prepare for his First Communion, and during the
third and fourth year for Confirmation.

Other Catholic leaders find serious flaws in this plan. They feel
that the first four years are psychologically more important for
the child's formation than the later years. They argue that, having started in one kind of school, the children would find it trying
to transfer to another. Moreover, many parents would find the

[10] New York *Times,* April 8, 1959.

budgetary adjustment from tax-supported to tuition-supported schooling impossible to make.

The above dilemma brings out one point clearly. If a larger proportion of Catholic children are to receive Catholic education during the years immediately ahead, the financial support of the schools must go beyond the contributed services of the religious and priest faculties and the tuition payments of school parents. To raise money for new schools and their operation, more and more dioceses are levying taxes on all parishes for the diocesan school fund. In order to build needed high schools, one large diocese assessed every parish 20 per cent of its gross income for each of five years. This diocese can now accommodate every Catholic boy or girl of high school age.

In adjusting the ideal to the demands of the present a bishop or pastor must weigh all the educational and pastoral factors involved and then decide alternatives. Local conditions many times justify temporary compromises that may not be in perfect accord with either the Catholic ideal of education or standard academic practices. At least the pastor's school housing problem is shared by thousands of sincere public school administrators who can sympathize with him.[11]

How large a place does the teaching of religious doctrine occupy in a Catholic school? The average parochial elementary school devotes a 30-minute period daily or a weekly total of 150 minutes to the formal teaching of religion. In the high schools there is greater variety in the length and number of class periods. Many schools have a daily 30- or 40-minute period which also includes provision for related activities. Other high schools allot two 45-minute periods or three 30-minute sessions weekly. Religion, as a curricular subject, includes not only Christian doctrine or catechism but a study of the Bible and church history. On the secondary school level it also commonly includes apologetics and

---

[11] Most dioceses, however, have strict regulations to limit class size. The merits of large or small classes have been much discussed, but no one has found the final answer. The NEA urges an optimum class size of 25 pupils. Discussions of the NCEA have favored a figure of 35. In any event, population pressures, the use of teaching assistants, and individual pedagogic skill will continue to modify any ideal figure set up.

Catholic social teaching with emphasis on the encyclical letters of the Popes.

Though the Sisters and lay teachers themselves conduct the regular religion classes, wherever possible priests from the parish supplement this instruction by taking the religion period one day of the week. This is especially true in the upper elementary classes and in high schools. In the diocesan central high schools priest faculty members, as a rule, teach all the religion classes. Teachers of this subject have at their disposal the latest pedagogical techniques, teaching manuals, audio-visual aids, and other professional helps.

Do the religious activities of the parochial school interfere with the regular school work? Is there an imbalance in the curriculum between the time allotted to religion and secular subjects? There may be an individual school here or there in which some interference or imbalance exists, but these schools would be exceptional. Like their opposite numbers in public schools, parochial school administrators are keenly aware of pressures—many times from worthy sources pleading worthy causes—to alter the distribution of school time. Yet they are equally conscious of the responsibility of the school to preserve balance and accomplish all its appropriate tasks. And if a further reminder were needed there is always the knowledge that the school superintendent or religious community supervisor will have something to say about unauthorized departures from the syllabus and other regulations controlling the curriculum. Moreover, diocesan school authorities in regulating the distribution of school time conform to approved standard curricular practices.

What does a breakdown of time actually show in regard to the parochial school? The eighth-grade pupils in the school surveyed in the Fichter study spend 1,500 minutes a week in school, apportioned as follows:[12]

Religion	10.0%	Music	6.7%
English	37.3	Science and Health	5.3
Arithmetic	15.0	Art	4.0
Social Studies	16.0	Recess and Misc.	5.7

[12] Fichter, p. 106.

An allotment of two and one-half hours in a weekly total of twenty-five hours is hardly cause for concern that there is "too much" religion in the parochial school curriculum. There is a great deal to be said for the educative values of the religious study and activities that are scheduled. Far from being foreign to the purposes of the Catholic school, they serve as a firm foundation for the traditional Christian humanism which has civilized the Western world. Moreover, Catholic school products are, on the average, as highly regarded as their public school counterparts in the mastery of the skills and fields of secular knowledge measurable at either the start of high school or the beginning of college. Generally speaking, too, the parents of parochial school youngsters are more than satisfied with the blending of activities between the Church and the school and regard this integration as a valuable product of attendance at a Catholic school.

A great deal of misunderstanding and confusion exists concerning the attitude of the Catholic Church toward coeducation. Classroom separation of the sexes during certain years of biological and psychological growth, in addition to its sound moral basis, has also a firm pedagogical one. (Many leading academic institutions, secondary and collegiate, still follow the tradition of separate education for the sexes.)

The Catholic ideal calls for separate educational institutions for boys and girls, especially during the period of adolescence. This is clearly stated in the encyclical, "The Christian Education of Youth." When this ideal is not feasible, separate facilities are to be planned within the same institution, and when even this type of separation is impractical, school administrators are to provide additional supervision and separate instruction in certain fields.

Almost all public and parochial elementary schools in the United States are coeducational or coinstructional. In this the American tradition differs from that of some other countries. In the American grade school there is little or no distinction in the basic content of instruction, so that formal recognition is not made here of differing educational needs of boys and girls. Dangers and difficulties of the moral order become pronounced only with puberty which signals adolescent awareness of sex. With few exceptions children do not face these problems before the seventh grade. Nevertheless, parochial elementary schools follow some pattern of segregation by sex from the first grade on. When class size warrants it, there will be separate room sections for boys and girls of each grade. In a mixed class boys and girls are generally seated in sections on the two sides of the room, a pattern that perfectly parallels the children's own social inclinations or want of them. During the lunch hour and recess and recreation periods the segregation pattern is likewise preserved. Any attempt to force integration here, it might be added, would arouse indignation on the part of youthful hopscotch or baseball players.

The problem of coeducation is more serious on the secondary level. The ideal again is separate schools; a lesser ideal is separate classes in the same school; and full coeducation is tolerated only when circumstances leave no alternative. Circumstances, mainly economic, have forced a general modification of the ideal. In 1959 there were 2,349 Catholic secondary schools; slightly more than half, 1,240, were coeducational or coinstructional. Girls' high schools numbered 758, and there were 351 boys' high schools.

What are some of the reasons for the policy of segregation by sex? The obvious reason is the practical recognition this gives to the differences between the sexes. First of all, education does not prepare boys and girls to assume the same functions and careers in life. Boys and girls achieve biological maturity at a different tempo and manifest the stages of adolescence in different psychological ways. The consequent personal problems of self-consciousness, ideals, and friendships differ. Any experienced teacher can testify to the differences in motivation and pedagogical techniques that are required for effectively teaching boys and girls apart or together. Some subjects of the curriculum are ordinarily taught better to boys by men teachers and to girls by women teachers.

The moral training of adolescent boys and girls is best accommodated to these differences. Each sex is confronted during these years with new personal experiences of self and others, which must, in the words of an eminent Catholic sociologist, "be properly interpreted, gradually mastered and soundly integrated into the total development of each one's personality."[13] During this

[13] Rev. John L. Thomas, S.J. Father Thomas discusses this problem in *The American Catholic Family*, a model of scholarly sociology.

period of rapid growth boys and girls first become aware of the personal power of sex, whose mastery requires, in addition to self-knowledge and self-discipline, a considerable length of time. It does not make good pedagogical sense to increase the association of boys and girls with one another before they have had time to understand and grow into this new responsibility.

Even those who build their theory of education on a purely natural plane with no reference to the Christian doctrines of original sin and grace, can discover empirical validity here for at least partial segregation of the sexes during the emotionally charged years of adolescence. Catholic educators and parents are by no means alone in their concern for certain trends among modern youth that arise from the unsupervised mingling of the sexes. These trends would include pre-teen dating, going "steady" among teen-agers, all-night partying, use of alcohol, and indecent entertainment.

The objection is sometimes made that sexually segregated education is unrealistic. If the school should prepare young people for life, these critics argue, it must teach them to make the adjustments between sexes that are necessary for adult life. One could reply that this is not the business of the school at all but belongs to the family and church. Furthermore, children are not yet adults, and it is a serious mistake, especially in what concerns sex, to treat them as if they were. The contacts between boys and girls during adolescence are best kept to what responsible society judges a proper minimum. Parental supervision is rendered extremely difficult when boys and girls spend the entire day side by side in the classroom and school activities.

From the Church's policy on coeducation it should not be concluded that the Church opposes social activities among adolescent boys and girls. On the contrary, Catholic high schools as well as parish young people's clubs sponsor a full program of activities which bring boys and girls frequently together under adult patronage.

We have previously discussed the theoretical rights of the church and the state in the field of education. In the practical order how do these two societies exercise their respective rights? The primary church laws presently governing Catholic education are contained in the revised *Code of Canon Law* which was promulgated in 1918. These canons or laws are the most authoritative expression of the mind of the Church in education and take precedence over all other types of ecclesiastical legislation.

The general principle of parental responsibility for education is stated in Canon 1113, in the section on the sacrament of matrimony: "Parents are bound by a most serious obligation to provide to the best of their ability for the religious and moral, as well as for the physical and civic, education of their children."

The Code treats in detail of the general teaching authority of the Church in the fourth part of Book III. Certain canons here discuss the schools. A few comments on the key passages will help toward understanding the Church's official position on the obligations and rights involved in education.

Canon 1372 recalls two elementary principles. The first half of the canon is simply a reminder of the natural law obligation that the faith and morals of children are to be protected, and that moral and religious formation must hold a paramount place in their education. The second restates a portion of Canon 1113 concerning the obligation of parents and of those who hold their place to provide a Christian education for their children.

The two parts of Canon 1373 contain the general prescription that children in school are to receive religious training:

1. In every elementary school children are to be given religious training proportioned to their age level.

2. Let young people who attend intermediate and higher schools be given a fuller training in religion, and let the local bishops make sure that this is done by priests conspicuous for their zeal and knowledge.

The next canon is the famous Canon 1374, one of the best known but least understood by non-Catholics in the entire Code. It reads:

Catholic children may not attend non-Catholic, neutral, or mixed schools, that is, those which are open also to non-Catholics. It pertains exclusively to the local bishop to decide, in accordance with instructions of the Holy See, under what circumstances and with what precautions against the danger of perversion, attendance at such schools may be tolerated.

The roots of this piece of legislation reach back into a stormy period of history. It was a period when the ideal of the "lay school" —which in practice was irreligious—prevailed in Europe, while in the United States, as we saw earlier, Catholics were trying to come to terms with America's unabashedly "Protestant" public schools. Earlier we quoted statements of the nineteenth-century American bishops, in which they warned Catholic parents of the dangers to the faith of their children that lay in attendance at these schools. But are there still grounds for this concern? Generally speaking, American public schools in the cities and the larger school systems can no longer be described as Protestant. The same, however, cannot be said of the schools in many small towns and in rural areas.

Moreover, as has been pointed out earlier, even the theoretical religious neutrality of the public school is based on assumptions which contradict Catholic belief. Some of these assumptions are indifferentism, or the acceptance of the equal claim to validity by all sects and churches;[14] private rather than institutional authority as the interpreter of faith and morals; and the infinite perfectibility of human nature through purely natural means. Granted the Catholic Church's firm convictions on these points, along with her concern over the secularism which today has so deeply penetrated the public school atmosphere, the Church's policy in legislating for the protection of her children's faith is not unreasonable.

In 1884 the Third Plenary Council of Baltimore drew up legislation requiring parishes to establish schools and parents to send their children to them. Penalties for noncompliance were included. The older American dioceses have long had their own regulations to supplement this general legislation, and since the 1918 revision of the *Code of Canon Law,* the same type of supplementary laws has been enacted or renewed in many dioceses. The particular

[14] Non-Catholics are free to look upon this dogmatic intolerance as a mass Catholic delusion, but a Catholic simply does not believe one religion is as good as another. Here there is no question of equal civil rights. An American Catholic holds the equality of all religions before the law. He respects the equal sincerity of each man's conscience. He honors the equal right that each man has to worship God according to his conscience. He respects the equal freedom that any man has, in fact, not to worship at all. But with this said, a Catholic still firmly believes that all religions are not equal in themselves. If he did not, there wouldn't be much point to his being a Catholic. This is a "constant" in the social picture, and is not susceptible to modification.

disciplinary decrees of the Baltimore Council and the Code itself are based on the moral principle that penitents who lack the proper disposition cannot be absolved. An Instruction sent by Pius IX in 1875 to the American hierarchy was drawn upon by the Council and the Code for this doctrine. The Instruction reminded the faithful that parents who consistently neglect to give the necessary Christian training and education to their children or who permit them to attend schools where spiritual ruin is inevitable cannot be absolved in the sacrament of Penance. This is all the more so in cases where there is a suitable Catholic school in the locality, or where parents have the means to send their children elsewhere to receive a Catholic education. The continuity and consistency of the Church's position over the past eighty-five years is shown by this modern example of diocesan legislation:

> Where a Catholic parochial school exists, parents ordinarily violate the general Canon Law of the Church (Canon 1374) if they send their children to public or non-Catholic schools. If they persist in this violation, they sin gravely and cannot be absolved until they make proper adjustment with the Ordinary through the Pastor.[15]

The natural law obliges parents to protect the spiritual and moral well-being of their offspring. Consequently, parents may not allow their children to frequent any places (schools included) where their faith and morals would be exposed to grave danger. When the Church reminds Catholic parents that attendance at a certain class of school can be dangerous for their children, she is primarily pointing out an obligation which already binds them in virtue of the natural law. Canon 1374 adds nothing to this natural obligation, except the provision that the local bishop is to approve exceptions to the general rule. Catholics accept this admonition, because they believe that the teaching office entrusted by Christ to the Church includes the right to clarify and interpret the natural law. A parent who continues to risk the welfare of his child is not properly disposed to receive sacramental absolution. When such a one repents and promises to perform his parental duty, he can be absolved.

---

[15] Statute 117, *Statutes of the Archdiocese of Indianapolis.*

In 1941 when Bishop Thomas J. Toolen of Mobile, Alabama, forbade the sacraments to those parents who sent their children to public schools, his action was commented on at length in a national news magazine. The bishop was quoted at the time as having said that only eleven of the Catholic dioceses of the United States enforced the "no absolution" rule for parents who failed to observe the canon law. A 1958 survey of diocesan school attendance regulations and their enforcement throws light on the current practice.[16]

The questionnaire upon which this survey was based was sent to 131 dioceses in the United States, and 104—almost exactly 80 per cent—replied. To the first question: "In your archdiocese or diocese is there a statute requiring Catholic parents to send their children to a Catholic school?", the answers were:

Yes: 55
No: 49

In the Yes category were also included replies which simply stated that the canon law of the Church was enforced or which reported episcopal regulations.

A further question was asked: "If there is no statute such as mentioned in Question 1, are there restrictions or regulations of any kind concerning attendance of Catholic children at public schools?" The responses:

Yes: 9
No: 40

The affirmative answers stated that the diocesan regulations simply repeated the prescriptions of canon law and the Third Plenary Council of Baltimore, or that there were simple episcopal decrees.

Another question asked: "If there is such a statute, do these Catholic parents who defy it incur a reserved sin?" (A "reserved" sin is one whose absolution must be sought directly or indirectly from the local bishop.) The answers were:

Yes: 12
No: 43

16 The author is indebted to Rev. Daniel M. Kirwin, superintendent of schools of the Diocese of Wheeling, West Va., for making the results of his private survey available to readers of this book.

The questionnaire also inquired as to the extension of the diocesan statute: did it apply to attendance at elementary schools only, or secondary schools only, or both? Seven dioceses apply the statute only to elementary schools, no diocese limits it to secondary schools, and 48 apply it to both levels of education. Moreover, nine dioceses volunteered the information that their statutes also cover attendance at colleges and universities, while three require permission for attendance at sectarian colleges.

These were the responses to the question, "If there is such a statute, must parents formally apply for permission to send their children to a public school?":

Yes: 38
No: 17

Briefly then, 55 of 104 dioceses in the survey require attendance at a Catholic school, either through diocesan statute or episcopal order. Nine other dioceses, however, have some restrictions or regulations governing attendance of Catholic children at public schools, but formal permission for this is required in only 38 dioceses. Failure to send children to the Catholic school *can* result in 12 dioceses in the denial of absolution to recalcitrant parents. Instances of enforcement of this penalty, however, seem to be so rare that they still provide copy for *Time* magazine.

The remarks accompanying the questionnaire confirm this observation. Because almost no diocese has sufficient educational facilities to cope with the demand for Catholic schooling, diocesan regulations are not strictly enforced. Where permission to attend a public school is mandatory, the permission is given only with the assurance that the child will be enrolled in religious instruction classes. In those dioceses where no formal legislation requiring attendance at Catholic schools exists, parents are reminded of their duty in sermons and in the diocesan press. Most dioceses that do require permission for children to attend a public school admit that this requirement is not well observed.

The Code itself intimates that there are exceptions to the compulsory-attendance law, which are within the competence of the bishop to approve. On this point the Third Council of Baltimore itself quotes the 1875 Instruction of the Holy Office, stating that "it will usually be a sufficient reason if there is either no

Catholic school at all available, or only one which is inadequate for the suitable education of the children according to their condition." Suitable means to avoid perversion of faith were, however, still to be taken.

The 198th decree of the Baltimore Council illustrates the caution with which the bishops approached the delicate problem of sanctions:

> If therefore, for a sufficient reason approved by the Ordinary, Catholics wish to send their children to the public schools, provided the proximate danger be made remote by taking the necessary precautions, we strictly forbid, as the Supreme Pontiff through the Sacred Congregation has expressly forbidden, that any Bishop or priest either threaten to exclude such parents from the reception of the Sacraments, or actually so exclude them. And much more is this to be understood of the children themselves.

Canon 1374 on compulsory Catholic school attendance has prompted the charge in some unfriendly quarters that "the whole educational policy of the Church has been imposed upon Catholic people at the point of a theological gun." Let us look more closely at this claim.

The privilege of membership in the Catholic Church brings with it obligations of membership which are spelled out in the laws of the Church. Some of these laws carry a specially imposed sanction in the spiritual order, such as deprivation of the sacraments. When a Catholic refuses to follow such a law, he knows that he is freely cutting himself off from communion with other members. The secular humanist, however, who no longer holds the traditional Christian notion of "sin," simply cannot grasp the concept of a sanction in the realm of conscience. He knows only the sanctions of physical coercion or of social pressure made use of in his world to enjoin group conformity. The secularist's indignation over the fancied plight of the poor Catholic is misdirected. If there is a "theological gun" pointed at his head, the Catholic knows it is there only as long as he freely wills it to be there. More important, he knows that if there were such a gun, he is the only one who could pull the trigger.

Other critics have called Canon 1374 a papal order for Catholic parents to boycott the American public school. The same criticism could be made of other canons. According to this way of thinking, Canon 1274 orders a boycott of Protestant churches by insisting that Catholics attend Sunday Mass in a Catholic church, and Canon 1252 orders Catholics to boycott butcher shops by requiring abstinence from meat on Fridays and Ember Days. The assumption upon which the "boycott" question rests is that Catholics must choose between a public school dedicated to producing American citizens and a religious school dedicated to producing Roman Catholics, whose falsity we have earlier shown. It is a strange reversal of the Christian and American tradition to assume that Catholics, or for that matter anyone else, have a primary allegiance to the state schools, so that in choosing to exercise their natural right to have their own schools they become guilty of disloyalty or of inflicting a boycott on the public schools.

Here are the last canons relevant to this part of our discussion. Canon 1375 asserts the right of the Church to found schools, and this right is elaborated upon in Canon 1379. If either elementary or secondary schools are wanting, "let there be provision for founding them, especially by the local bishops." Moreover, "if the public universities are not imbued with Catholic doctrine and thought, it is desirable that a national or regional Catholic university be established." The Catholic faithful likewise are reminded here to give a helping hand, according to their means, to the founding and support of Catholic schools.

Episcopal rights and responsibilities in education are the subject of Canon 1381.

1. The religious training of youth in all schools is subject to the authority and inspection of the Church.

2. The local bishops have the right and responsibility of watching out that nothing contrary to faith and morals be taught or take place in any schools within their territory.

3. Likewise, the bishops have the right to approve teachers of religion and religious textbooks; also, to demand the removal of either teachers or texts in the interests of religion and morality.

How does the state, in turn, exercise its educational rights for the common good? The complete and absolute separation of church and state would remove church-related schools from all accountability to the state, and render the state's police power inoperative as far as these institutions and their pupils were concerned. Only a few of the most doctrinaire advocates of the separation of church and state have pushed the logic of their position to this extreme. As we will see later, single states have exercised their regulatory power in the fields of health, safety, and morals for the general welfare of all students, no matter the type of school attended.

The state has, therefore, considerable control over the operation of Catholic schools. The law gives many administrative agencies of the state direct or indirect regulatory responsibilities for nonpublic as well as public schools. If nonpublic schools are conducted on a nonprofit basis, there is an appropriate state fiscal agency charged with their regulation. School buildings are subject to state supervision by agencies responsible for developing and enforcing building codes, fire regulations, health and sanitation codes, etc. Schools that employ workers are liable to regulation as employers of labor. Those schools that board and care for exceptional or handicapped children are subject to agencies charged with administering child welfare laws. Similarly, the operation of school buses comes under the agencies that administer the state motor vehicle code. The school cafeteria falls under the supervision of the state agencies responsible for administering the health and sanitation code. Nonpublic schools that are incorporated are subject to the regulations governing legal incorporation. And the list of examples could be extended.

A recent study of the supervision of church-related schools by the states, sponsored by the research division of the National Education Association, states that "three-fourths of the States provide by law that education in private schools shall be equivalent to the education given in public schools."[17] The legal provisions for achieving this aim vary from state to state, though in substance they resemble this Nebraska statute:

All private, denominational and parochial schools in the State

[17] *Research Bulletin,* Vol. XXXIV, No. 4 (December 1956), p. 208.

of Nebraska and all teachers employed or giving instruction
therein, shall be subject to and governed by the provisions of
the general school laws of the state as the same apply to grades,
qualifications, and certification of teachers and promotion of pupils. All private, denominational and parochial schools shall
have adequate equipment and supplies, and shall be graded
the same and shall have courses of study for each grade conducted therein, substantially the same as those given in the public schools where the children attending would attend in the
absence of such private, denominational, or parochial schools.[18]

The state laws governing compulsory education generally require (1) that all children between certain ages shall attend a
school; (2) which must be in session for a standard term; and
(3) which must provide the minimum educational program required by the state. The first two points are taken care of through
the reports on attendance that nearly all states require from every
school. Such reports based on the daily attendance records attest
that the pupils are complying with the compulsory education
laws. The minimum curriculum commonly includes mandatory
units in English, United States history and the history of the particular state, physical education, and social studies. Approval or
accreditation by the state department of education depends upon
the acceptance of these standards.

Nonpublic schools that voluntarily submit to state supervision
and that subsequently meet the state-established standards are
variously designated in different states. They may be called approved schools, accredited schools, or recognized schools, but
whatever the designation, they are officially acknowledged as institutions that are providing an educational program meeting
the minimum standards enforced in public institutions of similar
character.

The certification of teachers is another important control that
a state exercises over nonpublic schools. Some states make certification a requirement for teacher employment in all schools, public and nonpublic alike. Certification is required for nursery
school teachers in four states, for kindergarten teachers in six, for
elementary school teachers in nine, and for high school teachers

[18] Nebraska *Revised Statutes*, Sec. 79–1701.

in seven. More commonly, however, the states exercise an indirect control over the nonpublic schools by granting accreditation only to schools employing teachers who hold state-issued teaching certificates. This holds true in four states for nursery schools, in ten states for kindergarten schools, in nineteen states for elementary schools, and in twenty-two for high schools. State control through accreditation is the current trend.[19]

In general, state supervision of schools has resulted in improvement and maintenance of sound educational standards. From time to time it does happen that an individual state will succumb to pressures and tamper with curriculum content or teacher preparation in an arbitrary fashion. Educational theorists in state departments of education have a weakness for innovations, and the multiplication of "methods" courses for teacher certification is not the least harmful bit of their handiwork. Under the domes of some state capitols legal formulas have been conjured up to give the perfect classroom size, cubic yardage of air per pupil, and playground dimensions. The state's standardizing power is truly a formidable weapon to compel uniformity. It should be invoked cautiously lest the delicate balance of rights and responsibilities in education be upset.

[19] These figures are for 1957, the latest year surveyed. They were made available through the courtesy of the NEA research division.

CHAPTER 6

Parental Rights in the Courts

The Catholic theory of government is built on the age-old natural law. All men possess certain natural and inalienable rights which flow from the nature of man—rights which are not created by any state or by any constitution. These rights exist before states and constitutions come into being and will continue in unimpaired integrity when states and constitutions have passed into oblivion. Constitutions do not grant these rights, but register and guarantee them. The foundation upon which America's political institutions have been reared, the Declaration of Independence, asserts that these rights come to man, not from the state but from God, when it affirms that all men "are endowed by their Creator with certain unalienable rights, that among these are life, liberty and the pursuit of happiness." These rights are not held by grant of the state, but by grant of God. The state did not create them; it does not concede them; it may not destroy them.

Education is a good example of an area wherein a whole complex of rights and duties meet. Parents have the right and duty to educate their children according to the dictates of their conscience. The Church has the divinely conferred right to require its members to send their children to schools run under its auspices. The state, in turn, has a right to require parents to send their children to some school, or to educate them at home, so that the younger generation will receive the instruction it needs to become literate, responsible, and useful citizens.

It can be seen at once that the state would exceed its authority if it were to establish a compulsory system of public or common schools run by state officials at state expense, because such a system would inevitably conflict with the respective rights of parents and the Church to direct the education of their young. Throughout our history as a nation the courts have defended parental and religious rights in education. From the beginning there has been recognition of the principle that when the state establishes schools, it is assisting the parent and not replacing him, that the rights of the state in education are secondary and derived from parental delegation.

As early as 1842, the Supreme Court of Pennsylvania, after pointing out that the term "education" is not limited to the ordinary instruction of the child in the pursuits of literature but that "it comprehends a proper attention to the moral and religious sentiments of the child," declared that "in the discharge of this duty it is the undoubted right of the father to designate such teachers, either in morals, religion or literature, as he shall deem best calculated to give correct instruction to the child." The Pennsylvania court further declared:

> No teacher, either in religion or in any other branch of education, has any authority over the child, except what he derives from its parent or guardian; and that authority may be withdrawn whenever the parent, in the exercise of his discretionary power, may think proper.[1]

The Supreme Court of Ohio in an 1877 decree stated that it is not "the public policy of the State that the children of the State shall not receive any education in any other schools than in one of the public schools established by itself."[2] In 1891 Kentucky added this provision to the Bill of Rights in its state constitution: "Nor shall any man be compelled to send his child to any school to which he may be conscientiously opposed."[3] A Kansas court attacked the declaration that "the rearing of children is a function which the state delegates to parents, and which it may resume at will, for its welfare through the welfare of the child." And in the same decision declared:

[1] *Commonwealth* v. *Armstrong* (1 Penn. Law Journal *Reports*, 146, 393).
[2] *Gilmour* v. *Petton*, cited in Carl Zollmann, *American Church Law* (St. Paul: West Publishing Co., 1933), p. 92.
[3] See *America*, July 30, 1938, p. 395.

The rearing of children is not in fact a function delegated by the state to the citizens, any more than the begetting of children is a delegated state function, and the theory of government recognized by the declaration is responsible for absolutism in its most tyrannical form. The theory is expressly repudiated by the first two sections of the Bill of Rights of this State.[4]

Despite the legal tradition, attempts have been made periodically to impose a single compulsory system of education upon the country, usually under the plea that the times demand a "stronger" democratic unity or a "purer" Americanism. Thus far, all efforts in this direction have foundered in the courts. The U. S. Supreme Court has handed down several notable decisions since 1920, giving formal recognition to the educational and religious liberty of the family. The high court has consistently recognized that freedom to educate and freedom to worship are inseparable. The two most important cases decided by the U. S. Supreme Court on this point are *Meyer* v. *Nebraska* and *Pierce* v. *Society of Sisters*, better known as the Oregon school case. Both merit careful consideration for the light they bring to present school problems.

The nationalist hysteria which rose during World War I and its aftermath turned particularly against the German-language schools and the teaching of German in public schools. A sad commentary on these years is the fact that between 1917 and 1921 thirty-one states passed legislation requiring all instruction in the public schools to be given in English. A law passed by Nebraska in 1919 went further. It forbade instruction in any language except English in all schools, private as well as public. Under this law, a court convicted Robert T. Meyer, a teacher in a parochial school sponsored by the Zion Evangelical Lutheran Church, of having taught a ten-year-old child to read in German through use of a collection of Bible stories.

The Nebraska Supreme Court upheld the finding of guilty, but was itself reversed by a 7–2 decision of the U. S. Supreme Court. Justice Oliver Wendell Holmes dissented on the principle that he "was not prepared to say" that the Nebraska law "was unreasonable," and in this dissent he was joined by Justice George

[4] *Denton* v. *James*, cited in *Oregon School Cases: Complete Record* (Baltimore: Belvedere Press, 1925), p. 324.

Sutherland. Though the immediate issue was the liberty of a citizen to pursue his livelihood by entering into a contract to teach, something greater was at stake: the right of parents to control the education of the child. By way of corollary this involved the legality of private and parochial schools to exist in competition with the public schools. Arthur F. Mullen, a prominent Catholic attorney of Omaha, Nebraska, made the freedoms guaranteed to all United States citizens by the Bill of Rights the basis of the Meyer defense.

The exchange between Justice James C. McReynolds, who was to write the decisions in this and the Oregon school case, and Mr. Mullen helped isolate the critical point.

Q. (Justice McReynolds interposing) I just want to see what you claim. What about the power of the State to require the children to attend the public schools?
A. That is what I will come to in a moment.
Q. You will admit that, will you not?
A. I do not admit that.
Q. You do not admit that?
A. I do not admit that. I deny that a State can, by a majority of the legislature, require me to send my child to the public schools. I submit this, however: I agree with the proposition that under the police power, the State has authority to regulate private schools. I distinguish between the right to abolish an institution and to regulate it.[5]

After further questioning, in which Chief Justice William Howard Taft joined, Mr. Mullen proceeded.

It is not seriously argued that a legislative majority can, by its mere fiat, take my children and require me to send them to a public school, and have the course of study absolutely controlled by the State. I deny that any such power exists in a constitutional government.

That question is at the very base of this case. It is a blow at education; it is striking down the principle that a parent has control over the education of his child. I deny the power of a legislative majority to take the child from its parents.

[5] Quoted in *America*, July 30, 1938, p. 395.

These important questions have been discussed here very quickly. The right of a man to communicate with his family, and the right of a man to give religious instruction to his children; the right to be free in his home; the right to maintain private educational institutions, and in these matters to be let alone—surely these are "privileges and immunities" protected by the Constitution of the United States. And these rights should not be fixed or limited by narrow and devitalized definitions of constitutional liberty.[6]

Mr. Mullen's cogent presentation persuaded a majority of the justices. The opinion delivered by the court on this occasion was to furnish the basis of the even more significant Oregon school case which was decided two years later.

While agreeing in the Meyer case that "the state may do much, go very far, indeed, in order to improve the quality of its citizens, physically, mentally and morally," the Supreme Court affirmed that "the individual has certain fundamental rights which must be respected. The protection of the Constitution extends to all—to those who speak other languages as well as to those born with English on the tongue." The court did not deny that "perhaps it would be highly advantageous if all had ready understanding of our ordinary speech, but this cannot be coerced by methods which conflict with the Constitution. A desirable end cannot be promoted by prohibited means."

The great modern charter of parental rights in education is the unanimous decision of the U. S. Supreme Court in the Oregon school case. In 1922 the state of Oregon adopted by popular referendum—the vote was 115,000 to 103,000 roundly—a law requiring that all children between the ages of eight and sixteen be sent to a public school. There were exemptions listed in the law for children who were not normal, or who had completed the eighth grade, or who resided at considerable distances from any public school, or whose parents held special permits from the county superintendent. Failure to comply was punishable as a misdemeanor, and each day's failure to send a child to a public

6 Ibid.

school was to constitute a separate offense.[7] The law was to take effect September 1, 1926—but it never did.

The Society of the Sisters of the Holy Names of Jesus and Mary, an order of teaching nuns that conducted a number of Catholic parochial and private schools in the state, along with the Hill Military Academy, a privately incorporated nonsectarian school, obtained an injunction in the federal district court. Oregon state officials were thereby enjoined "from threatening or attempting to enforce the Act" which the panel of three judges constituting the court found to be unconstitutional.

The court ruled that the Fourteenth Amendment guaranteed appellees against the deprivation of their property without due process of law. It declared the right to conduct schools was property and that parents and guardians, as a part of their liberty, might direct the education of children by selecting reputable teachers and places. Also, that "these schools were not unfit or harmful to the public, and that enforcement of the challenged statute would unlawfully deprive them of patronage and thereby destroy their owners' business and property." The attorney general of the state of Oregon, acting in the name of Governor Walter M. Pierce, appealed at once to the Supreme Court of the United States.

Few people any longer bother to turn the hundreds of pages which make up the record of the Oregon school case.[8] This is the more unfortunate in that questions raised today about the relationship of parental freedom of choice to state-supported compulsory education and of private to public schools were answered a generation ago. It is appalling how superficially these historical documents are treated in some histories of American education and ignored in articles discussing the American philosophy of education by those writers who seek to aggrandize public education. The briefs and oral discussion presented by both sides in the Oregon case contain just about every argument conceivable in favor of and in opposition to nonpublic schools.

---

[7] The penalties: ". . . a fine of not less than $5, or more than $100, or to imprisonment in the county jail not less than two nor more than thirty days, or by both fine and imprisonment in the discretion of the court."

[8] The best compilation of the briefs and proceedings is *Oregon School Cases: Complete Record* (Baltimore: Belvedere Press, 1925), 943 pp.

In presenting its case the state of Oregon laid stress on the point that parochial and private schools were an anachronism, stating: "The necessity for any other kind of school than that provided by the state has ceased to exist. The public school is everywhere recognized as being an institution vital to the welfare of the individual citizen, and to that of the state and nation."[9]

Moreover, the state argued that the continued existence of nonpublic schools could prove a fatal menace to the public school system. The specter was drawn in these words:

> If a few such institutions can lawfully be maintained on behalf of the different religious denominations, the number which may ultimately be so maintained cannot consistently be limited, and if this court should hold that the state does not have the right to require all children within its borders to be educated in its public schools, religious denominations may, without constitutional restrictions, develop a system of educational training which will result in doing away with public schools.[10]

Religious schools were not only anachronistic and a menace, but they were divisive and undemocratic. The state counsel asked why children were placed in parochial schools at all and deprived of "the benefits of a public school education which follows from association of children with others of their own age and kind." He answered his own question: "There can be but one answer. It is to stamp upon its children a distinction which is to set them apart during the rest of their lives, and to make them other than they would be if they grew up in the atmosphere of the democracy of the public schools."[11]

The Oregon brief pleaded the necessity of democratic unity, a benefit which could only be obtained through a single system of state schools.

> Our children must not under any pretext, be it based upon money, creed or social status, be divided into antagonistic groups, there to absorb the narrow views of life as they are taught. If they are so divided, we will find our citizenship composed and made up of cliques, cults and factions each striving,

9 Ibid., p. 200.
10 Ibid., p. 202.
11 Ibid., p. 690.

not for the good of the whole, but for the supremacy of themselves. A divided school can no more succeed than a divided nation.[12]

Another argument officially advanced to justify the Oregon school measure was that if the states have no power to provide for the education of the children within their territories, and if the character of the education of such children is to be entirely dictated by the parents of such children, or by those persons by whose influence the parents are controlled, "it is hard to assign any limits to the injurious effect, from the standpoint of American patriotism, which may result." One of the horrendous examples of what could happen to the Oregon children was that they might be taught "that the claims upon them of the religion to which they belong are superior to the claims of the United States."[13]

Further proof of the essentially religious aspect of the freedom at stake is to be found in this statement of the State's brief, that "in its last analysis, the argument of appellee is that it demands, as a right guaranteed under the Constitution of the United States, the right to conduct an institution for the instruction of children of common school age in opposition to the public schools maintained by the state, *in order that it may therein give sectarian religious instruction which is prohibited in the public schools.*"[14]

As far as the Catholic conscience is concerned, the clash of basic educational philosophies was nowhere better illustrated than in the oral argument before the Supreme Court, presented on behalf of the state by Oregon's Senator George E. Chamberlain, a former attorney general and twice-elected governor of that state:

Between the church itself and the state, we insist that the state has the prior and paramount right to direct the education of the children of the state.

I question the right of the Catholic, or any other church, to insist that its communicants and adherents have the absolute right to send their children wherever they please to be educated in the elementary grades, and I challenge the statement, that there is any liberty to the parents or to the children under

12 Ibid., p. 272.
13 Ibid., p. 116.
14 Ibid., p. 202. (emphasis added)

the rules of the church. As between the two, the church and the state, the state has the paramount right.[15]

The oral arguments were heard by the Supreme Court on March 16 and 17, 1925. The following June 1, Mr. Justice Mc-Reynolds delivered the court's opinion. By a unanimous decision the lower court ruling of unconstitutionality was upheld. There was no question, ruled the court, of the State's power "reasonably to regulate all schools, to inspect, supervise and examine them, their teachers and pupils; to require that all children of proper age attend some school, that teachers shall be of good moral character and patriotic disposition, that certain studies plainly essential to good citizenship must be taught, and that nothing be taught which is manifestly inimical to the public welfare."

The court pointed out that enforcement of the Act would destroy "appellee's primary schools, and perhaps all other private primary schools for normal children within the State of Oregon." Furthermore,

These parties are engaged in a kind of undertaking not inherently harmful, but long regarded as useful and meritorious. Certainly there is nothing in the present records to indicate that they have failed to discharge their obligations to patrons, students or the State. And there are no peculiar circumstances or present emergencies which demand extraordinary measures relative to primary education.

Negative though this compliment to the civic usefulness of private education was, there were many devotees of a state monopoly of education who would not grant it.

"Under the doctrine of *Meyer* v. *Nebraska*," continued the court, "we think it entirely plain that the Act of 1922 unreasonably interferes with the liberty of parents and guardians to direct the upbringing and education of children under their control." And then the court uttered these memorable words:

The fundamental theory of liberty upon which all governments in this Union repose excludes any general power of the State to standardize its children by forcing them to accept instruction

[15] Ibid., p. 683. The Church does not claim an "absolute" right. See Chapter 4.

from public teachers only. The child is not the mere creature of the State; those who nurture him and direct his destiny have the right, coupled with the high duty, to recognize and prepare him for additional obligations.[16]

The Oregon school bill, originally proposed by the Scottish rite Masons, became a pivotal issue in the elections of 1922. His opposition to the measure, according to many observers, led to the defeat of Governor Ben W. Olcott. From the moment of its passage the bill attracted national attention, for the forces that brought it to the ballot and made Oregon a religious battleground were active in other states. Voters in California, Oklahoma, and Washington were asked to vote on school measures similar to that of Oregon. Michigan voters twice, in 1920 and 1924, rejected a compulsory public school law.

The American press was almost unanimous in its criticism of the Oregon bill. Commenting on the bill's passage in the 1922 election, the Louisville *Herald* editorialized: "In plain fact the outcome is to be accounted a victory for the Klan, a direct outcome of the campaign conducted by the Ku Klux organization, not less influential and not less illiberally active in the Northwest than in the South." The same paper identified the intent of the bill: "The purpose was quite unmistakable and to put a gloss on it is to indulge the pseudo-patriotism of these self-appointed guardians of our institutions. That purpose was to crush the parish schools of the Catholics. . . ."[17]

The New York *Times* declared that the nearest analogy to the Oregon law "is to be found in Russia under the present regime, and in Turkey under a bill which proposed specifically to prohibit attendance upon other than schools conducted by the Government. The law partook also of the spirit and method of the Prussian educational system."[18] The St. Louis *Post-Dispatch* said: "This Oregon law is above all else . . . an un-American attempt

[16] Historians of education have been derelict in treating the Oregon case. Canon Stokes writes: "It is specially significant as being decided on its constitutional merits when this country was at peace, and before Nazi totalitarianism made its threat against the United States." *Church and State in the United States*, II, 741.

[17] November 18, 1922.

[18] April 2, 1924.

to take away the constitutional right to liberty of conscience under the guise of zeal for education."[19] Writing under date of November 3, 1923, the editor of the Portland *Oregonian* bade his fellow citizens note that the law was something even worse than an attack on religious liberty. It is, he wrote, "a forthright declaration that the state, not the parent, controls the child. It is nothing else, and it is not pretended that it is anything else."[20]

All this is a matter of record, and the virulent anti-Catholicism whipped up by leaders of Masonry and the Ku Klux Klan deeply divided Oregon then and for years afterward. Electioneering materials of the crudest sort appeared everywhere. Fiery crosses burned at Klan meetings throughout the state. Catholic nuns were jeered at in the streets of Portland and church property was threatened.

The Oregon school bill was initiated and officially sponsored by the Masonic lodges of the state of Oregon. The group of men whose names appeared on the official ballot as sponsors of the initiative petition were high-ranking officials and members of Masonic groups. These men prepared and signed the formal argument in favor of passage printed on the official ballot. They concluded their printed argument with the acknowledgement that the "inspiration for this act" was a resolution adopted in May, 1920, by the Supreme Council, A. & S. Rite, for the southern jurisdiction of the United States; in June, 1920, by the Grand Lodge of Oregon, A.F. & A.M., and by the Imperial Council, A.A.O. Nobles Mystic Shrine.[21]

Governor Pierce and other state officials adopted a curious position during the trial in the federal district court which first de-

[19] April 1, 1924.
[20] Ibid.
[21] Here is the resolution: "*Resolved*, That we recognize and proclaim our belief in the free and compulsory education of the children of our nation in public primary schools supported by public taxation, upon which all children shall attend and be instructed in the English language only without regard to race or creed as the only sure foundation for the perpetuation and preservation of our free institutions, guaranteed by the Constitution of the United States, and we pledge the efforts of the membership of the order to promote by all lawful means the organization, extension and development to the highest degree of such schools, and to oppose the efforts of any and all who seek to limit, curtail, hinder or destroy the public school system of our land." (Quoted in *Oregon School Cases*, p. 733.)

clared the unconstitutionality of the school bill. Though the defendants cited by name in this trial were the governor, the attorney general of the state, and the district attorney of Multnomah County, the case was openly argued as a Masonic crusade. Mr. Wallace McCamant, attorney of record for the state of Oregon, announced at the outset: "I appear here primarily as the representative and at the instance of the Scottish rite Masonic bodies."

The open display of religious bigotry by state officials shocked and dismayed Americans throughout the nation. The Oregon bill was denounced in dozens of speeches and resolutions. Formal protests were published by sympathetic Protestant and Jewish groups. *Amicus curiae* briefs were entered in the Supreme Court trial by the Protestant Episcopal Church, the Seventh-Day Adventists, and the American Jewish Committee. In the lead editorial for June 2, 1925, the New York *Times* commented:

> Yesterday's decision by the Supreme Court holding invalid the Oregon School law is none the less welcome for being expected. The statute set aside was born of prejudice. . . . The measure professed to be one of equality, but it was plainly directed most intolerantly at a single class. It was one of the most hateful by-products of the Ku Klux movement, which now happily seems to be dying out.

Writing thirty years later an historian of American church-state relations could hail the Oregon school case decision "as one of the wisest and most important decisions of the Supreme Court in voiding a state law as unconstitutional."[22] The court's ringing reaffirmation of religious liberty and educational freedom is truly a landmark, and the *Pierce* v. *Society of Sisters* case has been cited over and over in judicial decisions dealing with parental liberties.

The parents' right to direct their child's education is part of freedom of religion. This was the issue in two compulsory flag-saluting cases which involved children of Jehovah's Witnesses. These people look upon the practice of flag-saluting as idolatrous. In the first case, *Minersville* v. *Gobitis* (1940), the majority opinion admitted that there was great diversity of psychological and

[22] Stokes, *Church and State in the United States*, II, 741.

ethical opinion concerning the best way to train children for their place in society. In fact, because of these differences and the court's reluctance "to permit a single, ironcast system of education to be imposed upon a nation compounded of so many strains, we have held that, even though public education is one of our most cherished democratic institutions, the Bill of Rights bars a State from compelling all children to attend the public schools." The precedent cited was *Pierce* v. *Society of Sisters*.[23] Nevertheless, the court decided that the Minersville school board could compel children to salute the American flag, as a proper means of inculcating national unity.

Justice Harlan F. Stone was the lone dissenter in the *Gobitis* case. He, too, appealed to the precedent set by the *Pierce* decision, but went further than his colleagues in facing the implications therein. The religious liberty of parents and their freedom to educate according to conscience, he wrote, had to be protected against the compulsory power of the state. Regarding the flag-salute itself, the justice said, "Even if we believe that such compulsions will contribute to national unity, there are other ways to teach loyalty and patriotism which are the sources of national unity, than by compelling the pupil to affirm that which he does not believe and by commanding a form of affirmance which violates his religious convictions."

Three years later, a second compulsory flag-saluting case, *Barnette* v. *West Virginia* (1943) reached the Supreme Court. Now, however, the majority, in overruling the *Gobitis* decision, followed the direction pointed out by the earlier Stone dissent. The *Barnette* decision warned of the latent tyranny in efforts by the state, as educator, to produce cultural conformity among its children. The very purpose of the Bill of Rights, the court said, was "to withdraw certain subjects from the vicissitudes of political controversy, to place them beyond the reach of majorities and officials. . . . One's right to life, liberty and property, to free speech, a free press, freedom of worship and assembly, and other

[23] A clear echo of the wording of the *Pierce* case can be caught in this sentence from *Prince* v. *Massachusetts* (1944): "It is cardinal with us that the custody, care and nurture of the child reside first in the parents, whose primary function and freedom include preparation for obligations the state can neither supply nor hinder."

fundamental rights may not be submitted to vote; they depend on the outcome of no elections." Accordingly, West Virginia could not require children of Jehovah's Witnesses to salute the flag.

Whether one agrees with it or not, Justice Felix Frankfurter's dissent in this case merits careful study, for the questions this dissent raised remain unanswered. The justice recalled that all citizens are taxed for the support of public schools, though in the *Pierce* decision the court denied the right of a state to compel all children to go to such schools and acknowledged the full right of parents to send their children to privately maintained schools. "Parents who are dissatisfied with the public schools," he admitted, "thus carry a double educational burden." The fact that children who go to public school "enjoy in many States derivative advantages such as free textbooks, free lunch and free transportation" raises the problem of consistency. Has American judicial opinion faced the corollary to parental freedom to educate according to religious convictions?

Mr. Justice Frankfurter himself raised these queries which will serve to introduce the next chapter:

> What of the claims for equality of treatment of those parents who, because of religious scruples, cannot send their children to public schools? What of the claim that if the right to send children to privately maintained schools is partly an exercise of religious conviction, to render effective this right it should be accompanied by equality of treatment by the state in supplying free textbooks, free lunch and free transportation to children who go to private schools? What of the claim that such grants are offensive to the cardinal constitutional doctrine of separation of Church and state?

Catholics will readily concede with Mr. Frankfurter that "these questions assume increasing importance in view of the steady growth of parochial schools both in number and in population."

CHAPTER 7

Governmental Aid to Nonpublic Education

Discussions regarding federal or state assistance for church-related education are peculiarly plagued by a fog of emotion. Slogans and metaphors are often made to do the work of rational argument. The classic example is the "wall of separation" which not only serves as a symbol dividing church and state, but which in recent years has been shutting off reasonable dialogue between groups of Americans that usually are quite ready to listen to one another on the subject of civil rights. The word "separation" is not even in the Constitution. It is Jefferson's word, and so is the wall, and when the two are taken together as the "wall of separation," we have, at best, a loose description of the historic pattern of American church-state relations.[1]

The metaphor of the "wall" is unfortunate, for the plain reason that no real wall can keep completely apart two institutions that largely share the same constituency and the same concerns for the common good. Even the word "separation" can be misleading.

The word "independence" more accurately describes the American system. It was in this sense that Jefferson's famous metaphor was used by Innocent XI a century before the United States became a nation. The French Church was struggling to maintain its independence in face of the encroachments of regal power, so the Pope wrote to Louis XIV of France:

Everyone sees what destruction and ruin, not solely in France but in the rest of the Christian world, would follow for the Catholic Church, what confusion of sacred and profane things,

[1] The expression first appears in a letter written by President Jefferson to the Danbury (Conn.) Baptist Association, January 1, 1802.

if the wall between the spiritual and the secular power were to be breached, with the influence of such an example spreading daily ever wider. In addition, unless so absurd and so certain an error is corrected a grave risk and danger to souls in this kingdom will result.[2]

Quite obviously, the wall that Pope Innocent XI was striving to uphold has little but the name in common with what some people are trying to build in America.

However, since the phrase, "separation of church and state," invariably enters into all discussions of the state's relation to religion and education, we have the charge of analyzing the concept to determine what it means and what it does not mean. Every American believes in some kind of separation of church and state, just as every American can be said to believe in the equally ambiguous phrase, "the American way of life." Certainly he would be an exception who would advocate the union of church and state or espouse "the un-American way of life." Controversy arises only when one declares his understanding of church-state separation or seeks an application of the principle to a given area of civic life.

In the present chapter we shall examine "separation" under these four headings:

1. The "no establishment" clause of the First Amendment and the attitude of the federal and state governments toward religion in American life.

2. The threat posed to religious liberty through failure to balance the "no establishment" clause with the "free exercise of religion" clause of the First Amendment.

3. The "religious qualification" test the government indirectly requires in the distribution of most of its welfare benefits.

---

[2] *Innocentii Pp. XI Epistolae ad Principes,* I, 225 (Romae: Typ. Vaticana, 1890). Here is the Latin passage: ". . . nemo non videt quae inde Ecclesiae Catholicae deformatio ac ruina, quae Sacrarum ac profanarum rerum confusio, sublato quodammodo inter spiritualem ac saecularem potestatem pariete medio, sit consecutura, non in Gallia solum, sed in omnibus aliis Christiani Orbis provinciis, manante in dies latius exempli auctoritate. Accedet ad haec, nisi error tam absurdus ac tam certus corrigatur, gravis iactura et periculum Animarum in isto Regno."

4. The various forms of state support for private religiously oriented undertakings, especially education.

There are two passages in the Federal Constitution which are the source of the doctrine of separation between church and state. The first sentence of the First Amendment, part of the American Bill of Rights, reads:

Congress shall make no law respecting an establishment of religion or prohibiting the free exercise thereof.

The Fourteenth Amendment, added after the Civil War, which in our generation has been interpreted by the Supreme Court as incorporating the guarantees of the First Amendment and extending them to the states, reads in part:

No State shall make or enforce any law which shall abridge the privileges or immunities of citizens of the United States, nor shall any State deprive any person of life, liberty, or property, without due process of law, nor deny to any person within its jurisdiction the equal protection of the laws.

Except for another brief passage in Article 6, Section 3 forbidding any religious test as a qualification for office, the U. S. Constitution is silent about religion or any relations between state and church. Why?

Commentators on constitutional history, from Joseph Story to Charles Warren and Edward S. Corwin, are agreed on the reasons for this almost complete silence concerning religion. First, there was no mention of religion because the federal government was to have no control over the subject, just as the document made no mention of education or intrastate commerce for a similar reason. Second, the people's religious beliefs and practices, as well as the extent of the control exercised over religion by the states, were so diverse that it was plainly impractical to attempt any uniform system of relationship between religion and government. It should be remembered that when the Constitutional Convention convened in Philadelphia in 1787, New York, New Jersey, Virginia, North Carolina, and Georgia had only recently discarded their state church; but Massachusetts, Connecticut, and New Hampshire still retained their Congregational Church and Maryland and South Carolina their Church of England establishment.

The debates in the various state conventions called to ratify the Constitution confirm the reasons for silence. What was the effect of the new United States Constitution? It forbade the new federal government to establish any church, and it likewise forbade it to place disabilities on any citizen in virtue of his religion. It did not lay the same restraints upon the states.[3] This development came only in 1868 with the ratification of the Fourteenth Amendment, according to the accepted legal interpretation today. This freedom for the states is proved by the fact that Connecticut did not disestablish the Congregational Church until 1818, Massachusetts not until 1833, and that New Hampshire by its state constitution to this day may legislate for "adequate provision . . . for the support and maintenance of public Protestant teachers of piety, religion, and morality."

James Madison, who proposed the First Amendment, was questioned by the Congress as to his understanding of it. The record reads: "Mr. Madison said, he apprehended the meaning of the words to be, that Congress should not establish a religion, and enforce the legal observation of it by law, nor to compel men to worship God in any manner contrary to their conscience." He answered further questions as to why such an amendment was needed with the comment, "He believed that the people feared one sect might obtain a preeminence, or two combine together, and establish a religion to which they would compel others to conform."[4]

Justice Joseph Story, the first great commentator on the Constitution, said that every American colony down to the Revolution, excepting possibly Rhode Island, "did openly by the whole course of its laws and institutions, support and sustain in some form the

---

[3] Two weeks before signing the Declaration of Independence, John Adams wrote: "I am for the most liberal toleration of all denominations of religionists, but I hope that Congress will never meddle with religion further than to say their own prayers, and to fast and give thanks once a year. Let every colony have its own religion without molestation." (Quoted in Stokes, I, 513.)

[4] *Annals of Congress*, I, 730. During his term as President, Madison proclaimed a national fast day to pray among other things, that "God would guide their public counsels," "animate their patriotism," and "bestow a blessing on their arms." Stokes, I, 491.

Christian religion." It would be fantastic to suppose that the day after achieving statehood, the new states individually or collectively intended to adopt a policy of hostility or even indifference to religion.

Some recent interpreters of the First Amendment, however, find in the "establishment of religion" clause an absolute prohibition against any co-operation on the part of the federal government (and because of the Fourteenth Amendment, the states, too) with the churches or religion, even when such co-operation is nondiscriminatory. This extreme view found temporary support in the definition of "establishment" given by the U. S. Supreme Court in the *Everson* case (1947), in which it was stated that "establishment" meant at least this:

> Neither a State nor the Federal Government can set up a church. Neither can pass laws which aid one religion, aid all religions or prefer one religion over another.

Certain passages in the writings of Jefferson and Madison have been appealed to as historical support for this interpretation. It is true that the attitude of both men, who were deists, toward institutionalized religion was not friendly. In their uncompromising opposition to church establishment, especially as it existed in their native Virginia, they made some strong statements, which have been put forward to prove their conviction that religion itself has no place in public life. On the other hand, they did speak in other statements for friendly co-operation between the state and religion. Granting certain ambiguities here, there is no doubt that during their terms as President, Jefferson and Madison did in general embody an officially co-operative attitude. In any event, there is no support for the theory of absolute separation in the public statements on the place of religion in civil society by George Washington, John Adams, Alexander Hamilton, John Hancock, and most of our early leaders, whose writings are often studiously ignored by those who are out to make a case for extreme separation.

Certainly the overwhelming majority of the citizenry in 1788, the year the states ratified the document, would have been shocked to learn that the new Constitution forbade the federal government to adopt a benign attitude toward religion. Justice Story has commented: "An attempt to level all religions, and to make it a matter of state policy to hold all in utter indifference would have created a universal disapprobation, if not universal indignation."

Any remaining ambiguity about the intention of the framers of the Constitution is resolved by even a cursory study of how the document was interpreted in practice. From the beginning, the federal and state governments have used public funds to support religion on a nondiscriminatory basis. The fact is unquestionable that on both national and state levels countless, literally countless, forms of co-operation between government and religion have been meshed into our political and social system.[5] The interpretation of absolute separation would require the dismantling of all these arrangements, some of them going back to the cradle days of the Republic. Even the proclamation of Thanksgiving Day each year by the President is an "aid" to religion. It contravenes the alleged neutrality between believers and nonbelievers. It requires money to publish the Thanksgiving Day proclamation which runs afoul of the alleged prohibition on the use of any tax, large or small, to support religious activities or institutions, whatever they may be labeled. Until the *Everson* case there had never been any serious acceptance of the claim that these practices violated constitutional separation of church and state or were the equivalent of an establishment of religion. It did happen, though, that in 1853 suit was brought on these grounds to eliminate the chaplaincies in Congress.

The Senate committee, appointed to study the charge, reported on the meaning of establishment in the minds of the framers of the Constitution, and explained:

It referred, without doubt, to that establishment which existed in the mother country, and its meaning is to be ascertained by ascertaining what that establishment was. It was the connexion with the state of a particular religious society, by its endowment, at the public expense, in exclusion of, or in preference to any other, by giving to its members exclusive political rights, and

[5] The most complete treatment of this subject is to be found in Richard J. Gabel, *Public Funds for Church and Private Schools.*

by compelling the attendance of those who rejected its communion upon its worship, or religious observances.[6]

The Senate committee defended the institution of congressional chaplains, denying that this constituted an establishment of religion, because no church or ecclesiastical association or system of religious faith thereby had introduced in its favor "all or any one of these obnoxious particulars—endowment at the public expense, peculiar privileges to its members, or disadvantages or penalties upon those who should reject its doctrines or belong to other communions."

In the judgment of many historians and constitutional lawyers, however, the Supreme Court in 1947 and 1948 backed away from our historical understanding of the First Amendment. The *McCollum* decision in 1948 outlawed the released-time program for religious instruction on public school premises, on the grounds presented in the *Everson* (1947) case; namely, that an establishment of religion meant that neither a state nor the federal government can pass laws which "aid one religion, aid all religions or prefer one religion over another." By co-operating, even on a nondiscriminatory basis, with the churches in giving religious instruction the state of Illinois was said by the court to have breached the high wall separating church and state.

The importance of the *Everson* and *McCollum* decisions makes it worth while to pause momentarily for a closer look at some background points. In the first case the U. S. Supreme Court sustained a ruling of the New Jersey State Supreme Court that a state transportation law which provided also for parochial school pupils was a violation neither of the state nor the Federal Constitution. In 1941 the New Jersey legislature had passed this law. Arch R. Everson challenged the legal right of the school board of Ewing under this statute to reimburse the parents of parochial school children. The township had authorized payment for the transportation of local students "to the Trenton and Pennington high schools and Catholic schools by way of public carrier." The favorable court decision was welcomed by Catholic educators, but the extreme separatist interpretation of the First Amendment under-

[6] *Reports of Committees of the Senate,* 32d Congress, 2d Session, (1852–53); Senate Report No. 376, January 19, 1853.

lying it caused anxiety. The following year the Supreme Court handed down its decision in the *McCollum* case and anxiety increased.

In 1945 Mrs. Vashti McCollum had sued in an Illinois court to test the legality of a voluntary religious instruction program in the Champaign public schools. As a secular humanist she wanted no part of the program for her ten-year-old son Terry. The religious instruction program, then in its sixth successful year of operation, was a joint undertaking of some fifty churches and synagogues. Pupils were admitted to the 30-minute weekly classes held inside the public school buildings only on the written request of the parents. No public funds were involved, all expenses being borne by the churches. After Mrs. McCollum's suit was rejected in the Illinois courts, it was appealed to the Supreme Court of the United States where it was upheld—and tolled the death knell for released-time religion classes in thirty-seven states.

The *McCollum* decision precipitated a national reaction which has been compared to the furor over the decision in the *Dred Scott* case. There was a national cry of dismay. The Attorney General of the United States deplored it and the *Journal* of the American Bar Association editorialized against it. The American Catholic hierarchy and many Protestant church groups criticized the decision which, in effect, decreed that "the public schools must be not only nonsectarian but secular or godless"—in Leo Pfeffer's words.[7] However, the McCollum ruling was not to endure for long and, in fact, as Dean Robert F. Drinan of the Boston College Law School has pointed out, during the four years of its life it was not used as the basis of any important ruling in American law.[8] The secularist philosophy reflected in the *Everson-McCollum* decisions sharply clashed with a venerable legal tradition and the instincts of the American people on the relations of government and religion. The court shortly returned to its own traditional position.

The 1952 *Zorach* decision of the Supreme Court did not so much as mention the "wall of separation" though it did formally profess adherence to the *McCollum* decision. In this case the court sustained the action of the New York City school board in providing

[7] Leo Pfeffer, *Liberties of an American* (Boston: Beacon Press, 1956).
[8] "Everson Case: Ten Years After," *America*, February 9, 1957.

a program for religious instruction which differed in one important particular from the Champaign program: the instruction was not given within public school buildings. Attorneys for Tessim Zorach and Esta Gluck, New York City taxpayers whose children attended public schools there, contended that this program was the same in essence as the one involved in the *McCollum* case. They argued that the influence of the school was put behind the religious instruction program, that public school teachers administered it, that the program interfered with normal secular instruction, and finally that the school served as a crutch upon which the churches leaned for support in giving religious training.

Justice Douglas, who wrote the 6–3 majority opinion in *Zorach,* carefully explained that the separation of the state from religion must not result in a relationship that is "hostile, suspicious and . . . unfriendly." The decision affirmed that "when the state encourages religious instruction . . . it follows the best of our traditions." The state may "encourage" religion, though it cannot aid it; the government should "sponsor an attitude" that lets each religious group flourish. There was no hint at the desirability of union between church and state. On the contrary, the court declared, there was not the slightest doubt that the First Amendment "reflects the philosophy that Church and state should be separated."

But the U. S. Supreme Court's great service here lay in isolating the precise areas of separation. How *absolute* is constitutional separation to be? The court stated:

> And so far as interference with the "free exercise of religion" and an "establishment" of religion are concerned, the separation must be complete and unequivocal. The First Amendment within the scope of its coverage permits no exception; the prohibition is absolute.

The pivotal question then is not, *Are* the religious prohibitions of the Constitution absolute? but rather, *In regard to what areas* are they absolute? The court answered that the First Amendment prohibition is absolute in regard to all measures (1) *respecting an establishment of religion* and (2) *prohibiting the free exercise thereof.*

The *Zorach* decision merely reaffirmed the traditional American understanding of our church-state tradition, in stating that the First Amendment "does not say that in every and all respects there shall be a separation of Church and state. Rather, it studiously defines the manner, the specific ways, in which there shall be no concert or union or dependency one on the other. That is the common sense of the matter." Were it otherwise the state and religion would be aliens to each other.

The court cited examples to show the absurdity of absolute separation. Churches could not be required to pay even property taxes. Municipalities would not be permitted to render police or fire protection to religious groups. Policemen who helped parishioners into their places of worship would violate the Constitution. Absolute separation would put an end to cherished traditions—prayers in our legislative halls; the appeals to the Almighty in the messages of the Chief Executive; the proclamations making Thanksgiving Day a holiday; "so help me God" in our courtroom oaths—these and all other references to the Almighty that run through our laws, our public rituals, our ceremonies would be flouting the First Amendment. A fastidious atheist or agnostic, the decision said, could even object to the supplication with which the court opens each session: "God save the United States and this Honorable Court."

Separation of church and state is one thing, but a state attempt to separate religion from its citizens is another. Even according to the pragmatic criterion of William James, traditional religion benefits the state. A democratic state has an evident concern that its members find "strong, living roots for belief in human dignity and freedom and for faith in the possibility of responsible self-government." The *Zorach* decision did not establish a church or all churches; it did more clearly establish religion as a factor—and a beneficent one—in the civic life of a nation.

One traditional way that the American governments have acknowledged the importance of religion as a beneficent factor in civic life is the tax exemption of educational, literary, and charitable institutions under church sponsorship. Jacques Barzun has pointed out that "it was the Founding Fathers—the men of letters who wrote the Declaration of Independence and the *Federalist Papers*—who laid it down as axiomatic that schools, churches and other institutions should be tax-free. They fastened the custom upon us like an immemorial law."[9] So natural is this that some states to this day have never bothered writing an explicit statute to cover the status of tax-exempt institutions.

The constitutions of thirty-six states, however, do contain explicit provisions under which the property of nonpublic schools can be freed from taxation.[10] Eight other states—Iowa, Maine, Maryland, Massachusetts, Michigan, New Hampshire, Rhode Island, and Vermont—have provisions in their constitutions calling for the encouragement of education. Several states—like Michigan, North Carolina, Ohio, and Nebraska—have based tax exemption on these well-known words of the Northwest Territorial Ordinance of 1787: "Religion, morality and knowledge being necessary to good government and the happiness of mankind, schools and the means of education shall forever be encouraged." New Hampshire and Massachusetts courts have upheld the granting of tax exemptions to nonpublic schools under constitutional provisions of this type. Tax exemptions may be provided by statute for certain classes of nonpublic schools without contravening the constitutions of Connecticut, Mississippi, Oregon, and Utah.

Absolute separation of Church and state would violate the First Amendment by seriously curtailing religious freedom, for the

[9] *The House of Intellect* (New York: Harper & Brothers, 1959), p. 178. The last of the 48 States to grant tax exemption to nonpublic schools on all levels of education was California. Though colleges and universities had been exempt since 1914, nonprofit high schools and elementary schools were accorded exemption only in 1951. California voters upheld the 1951 exemption law (passed by the State Assembly) in the 1952 elections. After long and wearying litigation the California Supreme Court received the case and ruled that the tax exemption was not unconstitutional. The U. S. Supreme Court refused to reopen the case, declaring that the California tax exemption presented "no substantial Federal question." The justices considered the issue settled once and for all; so did the California electorate which in 1958 was again called upon to vote on an initiative measure to impose taxation on nonpublic schools. The measure was overwhelmingly defeated by a ratio of more than two to one and a plurality of nearly two million votes.

[10] The most convenient source of references to the passages in the various state constitutions concerning nonpublic schools is *The State and Nonpublic Schools* issued by the U. S. Department of Health, Education and Welfare as Misc. 28 of 1958. An earlier compilation by the NEA is disappointingly incomplete and curiously "weighted." See *Research Bulletin* XXXIV, 4 (December 1956).

government must become involved with religion in order to pre-serve religious freedom. For instance, absolute separation which would bar the government from providing religious services on its ships and military reservations would result in a denial to citizens in the armed forces of opportunities for religious worship. Separa-tion must yield here to the free exercise of religion. The continual expansion of government activity makes it increasingly difficult for the government to avoid unintended restraints upon religious liberty. The large part assumed by federal and state action in areas of welfare and relief, education, public housing, and urban renewal makes it clearer than ever that attempts to maintain strict separation of church and state of necessity mean hostility to religion and unwarranted curtailment of religious freedom.

Separation of church and state has validity only as a means to an end. In other words, the principle of separation is instrumental and subordinate to the end envisioned—religious liberty. The con-cept of religious freedom will, accordingly, determine how much separation of church and state there ought to be. As Dr. Wilber G. Katz, former dean of the University of Chicago Law School, has said: "Separation ordinarily promotes religious freedom; it is defensible so long as it does, and only so long." And the same authority reminds those who would make separation an end in itself that "the basic American principle of Church-state relations is not separation but religious liberty." Religious freedom has its limits, but "they are not limits set by a principle of separation of Church and state."[11]

The classic case in point is the state in its relation to nonpublic school children. The state has passed compulsory school attend-ance laws, and to assist parents to comply with such legislation, has established a system of free public schools, but without any provision in them for religious training. In pursuit of the common good the state provides for its school children the substantial benefit of free education and certain auxiliary benefits related to education. However, a family seeking to follow simultaneously

[11] "The Case for Religious Liberty," in *Religion in America* (New York: Meridian Books, 1958), ed. John Cogley, p. 115. This book is a compilation of the papers delivered at a week-long Seminar on Religion in a Free Society sponsored by The Fund for the Republic in which the present writer partici-pated. For the clarification of several legal points in this chapter he owes thanks to Dr. Katz.

the dictates of conscience and the compulsory education law may not now, for all practical purposes, share in the state's provision for the common welfare. For, in the concrete, the state has set up what amounts to a religious test. Catholic parents, for reasons discussed at length in an earlier chapter, judge that in all conscience they cannot allow their children to attend the public school. If public benefits are so administered that citizens must do violence to their conscience in order to share in them, then the benefits are discriminatory. They are not truly public because to them is attached a religious qualification. That portion of the public which prefers to follow the dictates of conscience, fails to qualify (1) in general for the basic benefit of free education; (2) in most states for the bulk of the supplementary benefits given for the sake of the school child.

It is not the American way simply to dismiss this conscience as a private affair, a Catholic idiosyncrasy, and to let it go at that. Religious liberty and the constitutional prohibition of religious qualifications mean little unless, as Robert Henle has pointed out, "they relate to the precise peculiarities of each type of conscience. Hence our courts have shown a punctilious and precise concern to protect the consciences even of minorities commonly regarded as extremists. The court simply inquires what the conscience of the individual is; it does not judge that conscience *as a conscience,* but takes it into account as a *fact* and provides for it."[12]

Nor can the question be loftily waived with a statement, like that of Justice Rutledge in his *Everson* dissent, that "Like St. Paul's freedom, religious liberty with a great price must be bought. And for those who exercise it most fully, by insisting on religious education for their children mixed with secular, by the terms of our Constitution the price is greater than for others." This is preposterous. The last thing our Founding Fathers intended to do was to put a price tag on the religious liberty protected by the First Amendment that would put it beyond the reach of some citizens. The rights and freedoms guaranteed to American citizens in the Bill of Rights were intended to be common and personal. The equal protection guarantee, said the Supreme Court, "requires that all persons . . . shall be treated alike, under like circum-

12 "American Principles and Religious Schools," St. Louis University *Law Journal,* III, 3 (Spring 1955), p. 244.

stances and conditions, both in the privileges conferred and in the liabilities imposed."[13] Chief Justice Charles Evans Hughes stated elsewhere that "the essence of the constitutional right is that it is a personal one." It is "the individual who is entitled to the equal protection of the laws."[14]

The courts have made it clear that the government must leave parents free to send their children to schools of their choice. The corollary question here has been raised and answered in the affirmative by the former dean of the University of Chicago Law School: "Does the First Amendment permit the Government to respect that freedom further by arranging distribution of its various benefits so as to avoid discrimination against parents or students who make this choice?"[15] The same answer, Yes, has been given to this question by the courts, though they have not always applied it with consistency. The same majority decision of the U. S. Supreme Court in the *Everson* case that declared "no tax in any amount, large or small, can be levied to support any religious activities or institutions," solemnly warned: "We must be careful, in protecting the citizens of New Jersey against state-established churches, to be sure that we do not inadvertently prohibit New Jersey from extending its general state law benefits to all its citizens without regard to their religious belief."

The high court made it clear that fear of establishment must not lead to a restriction of constitutionally guaranteed freedom:

Other language of the First Amendment commands that New Jersey cannot hamper its citizens in the free exercise of their own religion. Consequently, it cannot exclude individual Catholics, Lutherans, Mohammedans, Baptists, Jews, Methodists, Non-believers, Presbyterians or the members of any other faith, because of their faith, or lack of it, from receiving the benefits of public welfare legislation.

These words of the U. S. Supreme Court have not been effectively heard in some states. Children in parochial schools are denied a share, or threatened with denial of a share, in the state's

[13] *Hayes* v. *Missouri,* 120 U. S. 68 (1887).
[14] *McCabe* v. *Atchison,* 235 U. S. 151 (1914).
[15] Katz, p. 109.

normal welfare program simply because they are in a parochial rather than a public school.

A few years ago, a nine-year-old girl attending Holy Cross parish school in Portland, Oregon, was sent by her parents to a public school for enrollment in a special class for children who are hard of hearing. The parochial school lacked facilities for instruction in lip reading and speech correction. The school district refused admission to her and three other children attending private schools on the ground that, under Oregon law, only children attending public schools had a legal right to such special instruction. In February 1954 a circuit court decision ordered the school board to admit the children to the special classes, because "it is bound by the long established duties of uniformity and equal protection."

The Board of Education of Decatur, Illinois, voted in August 1958 to restrict public nursing service to the public schools. Until a ruling by the attorney general of Illinois that such service was neither illegal nor unconstitutional, the six parochial schools of the city were deprived of public nursing service.

Bills in the state legislatures of Illinois and New York to include private and parochial school students in state-subsidized driver-training programs have been opposed in recent years by Protestant church groups, on the grounds that such programs were an aid to sectarian education.

In the fall of 1957 the ultimate in absurdity was reached. Dr. Abbott Book, executive director of the Northern California-Nevada Council of Churches, filed a complaint with the Board of Education of San Francisco that the employment of public-paid truant officers to enforce attendance of children in the parochial schools was "a complete violation of the separation of Church and state."[16]

In sum, failure to understand "no establishment" as a means to

[16] This aberration of common sense and decency falls into the same category as a 1952 suit in New Orleans. There the city had planned to erect in a public park a statue to honor Mother Francis Xavier Cabrini, recognized as a saint by the Catholic Church. This civic gesture was "in honor and recognition of the outstanding services rendered to the community in the field of child care and for her effort and sacrifices during the Yellow Fever epidemics of 1897 and 1905." Some vigilantes of the "wall" brought suit to have the statue removed, because its presence in a public park was a violation of the First Amendment! (*Singelmann* v. *Morrison.*)

achieve "free exercise" of religion destroys the equilibrium intended by the framers of the First Amendment. Moreover, the purpose of the First Amendment is frustrated in that its protection of religious freedom does not extend to citizens who wish to send their children to religiously oriented schools. At present these citizen-parents do not enjoy full freedom to direct the education of their offspring, but are forced to pay a price to implement the theoretical right that is theirs.

The usual rejoinder here is to repeat (1) that Catholics may share equally in the basic and supplemental benefits of publicly supported education by simply sending their children to the public schools, where they will be welcome; (2) that Catholics have every right to establish religious schools but they cannot expect any public support, for *that* would—and here is flourished the clinching argument—for *that* would violate the American tradition of separation of church and state. Within the somber shadow of that wall there is no place for further discussion. So the wall remains high, the public conscience is soothed, and each succeeding year the Catholic community feels itself more aggrieved.

What does governmental support of education mean? How do we determine the meaning of terms like "welfare," "benefit," "basic," "supplemental," "direct" and "indirect"? How do we arrive at decisions regarding the extension or application of these terms? Certainly there is nothing intrinsic to these concepts which will definitively settle the questions before us. History and sociology are perhaps more helpful here than principles of law or logic. In what concerns governmental help to education, tradition and approved practice vary widely from country to country and, within the same country, from period to period, for the meaning of the terms involved pretty well depends on what people want them to mean. As we shall see, it is difficult to find a uniform or consistent pattern of state aid to education even within our own United States. Before looking at the practices in the different states, however, it might be helpful to recall certain points.

The government encourages all schools, libraries, museums, hospitals, and similar institutions because their activities are recognized as a contribution to the total common good. Such institutions assist the state in the pursuit of its goal—the common welfare.

This principle remains valid even when an institution has a distinctive philosophical or theological orientation, or is under the supervision of clerical or religious trustees. The philanthropic nature of the activity, not the organizational structure of the sponsoring institution, is what the government takes cognizance of. The nature of the supporting legislation is determined by the primary purpose intended by the government and by the form in which it casts the law. For example, a college scholarship to a G.I. or a high school senior that incidentally works to the advantage of an institution in which he expends the scholarship funds, does not obscure the purpose of the state or alter the personal form of the benefit.[17] In other words, federal and state governments have recognized that it is impossible to so insulate a benefit to an individual citizen that no incidental benefits will accrue to some institution as well.

Even into the present century it was fairly common practice for the federal and state governments to give direct support—including both basic and supplemental aid—to private and church-related enterprises. Examples could be multiplied: colleges for Negroes, the Indian schools, the national leprosarium, institutes for the preparation of teachers, orphanages, hospitals, etc. The sectarian or private nature of the group sponsoring the activity was no obstacle because the service rendered was held to be a public benefit. Direct public assistance was given to schools through land grants, extension of credit, a share in state lotteries, even direct payments out of both the school fund and the common tax funds.

However, government subsidy is no longer given on the scale of former years. Federal and state subsidy, today, in the form of direct financial grants is in general limited to protective and eleemosynary institutions, notably to orphanages and hospitals. Public support here seems to present less the aspect of aid to a sectarian enterprise, and society is quicker to grasp the common welfare aspect of the work. Nonetheless, the principle of public service remains valid, and the theory would still justify direct sup-

---

[17] Those who argue that the G.I. Bill furnishes no precedent for the use of tax funds for private education must explain why the government should have more latitude in ignoring church-state separation when it distributes educational rewards for service than when it pursues exclusively educational purposes.

port of ordinary parochial and church-related schools—as is done in England and in many of the Commonwealth countries.

Another relevant factor in our discussion is the greater readiness of American society to approve indirect but substantial support for colleges and universities. Research grants, loans, fellowships, and scholarships to institutions of collegiate rank under church direction seem not to present the American public with the sectarian problem that exists on the lower levels of education.

The First Amendment prohibition against an establishment of religion forbids the use of public funds for strictly sectarian purposes, and the Fourteenth Amendment extends this injunction to the states. Society interprets this—as do the courts—to mean that ordinary general education undertaken by church groups is barred from most forms of tax assistance. In addition to these prohibitions from the federal Constitution, thirty-eight state constitutions contain provisions which explicitly deny public funds to sectarian schools or institutions. Fourteen state constitutions go further in prohibiting appropriations of money or property to schools or institutions under private control, whatever its nature. On the other hand, the constitutions of eight states— Alabama, Georgia, Maine, Nevada, New York, Pennsylvania, South Carolina, and Virginia—specifically authorize public aid to private schools or for educational purposes, under prescribed conditions.

Since 1819 Maine has provided authority in its constitution for the legislature "to encourage and suitably endow, from time to time, as the circumstances of the people may authorize, all academies, colleges and seminaries of learning within the State." The Pennsylvania constitution allows support for private normal schools established by law for the professional training of teachers for the public schools. New York allows the use of funds for the education and support of exceptional children in private and church-related institutions. In Nevada private corporations formed for charitable and educational purposes may be given public funds. In an effort to preserve a pattern of segregation in their school systems several southern states have adopted new statutory provisions which, if sustained by the courts, would make it possible to give direct subsidies to privately incorporated schools that are segregated and nonsectarian.

Classifying the forms of governmental assistance to education under sectarian auspices is not an easy task. Proponents of the "absolute separation" theory usually lump all benefits together into a single forbidden category. Some people do not even recognize the validity of certain categories of support. There is general acceptance, however, of the distinction between *direct* and *indirect* support to education. An outright grant of public land or money to a school is a form of *direct* support. It is likewise *basic* and *institutional.* A dental health program or a scholarship to a war orphan, on the contrary, is generally considered an *indirect* institutional aid. It is primarily a *personal* benefit for the recipient. These are clear instances which are widely accepted, but how does one classify tax exemption? And if property tax exemption is legitimate, is sales tax exemption? What about bus transportation, loans to schools and students, protective zoning regulations, and subsidized lunch programs? What, finally, is the child welfare principle?

Without attempting to define or to achieve precision in description, we might list what seem to be the basic categories into which federal and state support fall:

> Direct or Indirect
> Basic or Supplementary
> Personal or Institutional
> Economic or Socio-legal

It will be instructive to listen to what the courts have said about these categories. In the final chapter we shall try to pull together some conclusions relating to what is a reasonable Catholic position on welfare benefits and government support for Catholic schools.

The federal school-lunch programs originated during the depression years prior to World War II. In 1935 the Congress passed legislation to provide milk and hot lunches on a subsidized basis to the nation's school children in co-operation with the states. The purpose of the program, renewed and expanded by subsequent Congresses, is set forth in the 1946 Act: "It is the declared policy of Congress . . . to safeguard the health and well-being of the nation's children, and to encourage the domestic consumption of nutritious agricultural commodities and other food." Because many states interpret their constitutions as barring them from extending absolutely any type of support to nonsectarian or nonpublic schools, the federal government has set up a separate lunch program to cover these schools. In June of 1955 the Department of Agriculture was making cash payments directly to nonprofit private schools in twenty-seven states in which legal barriers prevented a state agency from doing so.[18]

Many states, including some that do not co-operate in the federal lunch program, through the state departments of education have assumed at least supervisory responsibility for some areas of health and safety for children in all schools. In New Hampshire, New York, Pennsylvania, and Rhode Island statutory provision is made for the physical examination of nonpublic school children under the general supervision of state departments of education. In Illinois, Maine, and Massachusetts public school officials are responsible for ensuring that persons having communicable tuberculosis are not employed in nonpublic schools. State departments of education in Oregon, Pennsylvania, and Rhode Island are required to oversee fire drills in nonpublic schools. In Washington public school officials are explicitly enjoined to see that school safety patrols are set up in nonpublic schools. In Maine and Michigan state education officials have specific statutory responsibilities for health and safety facilities in nonpublic school buildings.

In addition to the ordinary protection through police, fire, and sanitation service, the community provides its school children with other welfare benefits of a socio-legal character, without discriminating between public and parochial schools. School property is protected by zoning regulations because the community judges that school children might be harmed by the proximity of factory smoke, heavy trucking or taverns. The city will close off its streets during part of the day to form recreation areas for school youngsters. That is, public property is temporarily loaned

[18] The federal government in co-operation with the states has long had a subsidized program for vocational instruction. A survey made a few years ago by the State Board of Education of Connecticut showed that more than 40 per cent of the seventh- and eighth-grade children in private and parochial schools were receiving instruction in domestic science and industrial arts financed out of public funds. See Richard Joyce Smith, "Aid to Private and Parochial Schools," *America*, November 10, 1956.

to a sectarian institution to supplement its recreational facilities. Moreover, children from parochial as well as public schools are given preference in the use of public parks and playgrounds for organized class athletics and school team practice.

The principle justifying these programs is simply that the health and safety of the nation's children is a public concern, regardless of the school they happen to be attending. Moreover, it has long been accepted that the most convenient spot to gather children for medical and dental examinations is the school, and the most efficient way to administer such a program is through the school's administrative machinery. It taxes belief to realize that some states continue to exclude parochial school youngsters from these welfare benefits on the grounds of separation of church and state. The time may come when the federal government will be forced to step in and establish special clinics, hospitals, and cafeterias, where these children may be examined and treated for such things as dietary insufficiency or the effects of Strontium 90, as it now does during polio outbreaks. The state of its children's health is hardly a matter of indifference to the government. No one, moreover, has yet explained how a town or city can curb polio, eradicate tooth decay, or eliminate tuberculosis by confining its public health measures to children in the public school system.

A more controversial and less accepted application of the child-benefit principle is the supplying of textbooks to all school children indiscriminately. Eight states—Alabama, Indiana, Kansas, Louisiana, Mississippi, New Mexico, Oregon, and West Virginia—presently provide textbooks to nonpublic school children, though the Kansas, Indiana, and West Virginia statutes contain a needs test. The first "free textbook law" was passed in 1929 by Louisiana.[19] The statute was challenged but upheld as constitutional by

[19] The U. S. Office of Education estimates that one per cent of the school dollar goes for textbooks. The American Textbook Publishers Institute lists the following recommended expenditures for a set of books:

Grade	
1	$17.87
2	19.66
3	24.21
4	32.73
5	35.40
6	36.05

the Louisiana Supreme Court. Two suits were decided together. In the *Borden* case the court declared that children in parochial schools have a right to share in textbook programs, for the schools "obtain nothing from them, nor are they relieved of a single obligation, because of them. The school children and the State alone are the beneficiaries." The *Cochran* case, upheld by the Louisiana court in the same action, was the one appealed to the U. S. Supreme Court. On behalf of the court, Chief Justice Charles Evans Hughes rendered the court's unanimous opinion that the Louisiana law was constitutional.

The decision insisted that since the taxing power of the state is exerted for a public purpose, "the legislation does not segregate private schools, or their pupils, as its beneficiaries or attempt to interfere with any matters of exclusively private concern." The court's unanimous decision confirmed the principle that legislation is not void if it achieves a public purpose, even though in the process a private end is incidentally aided. The state's "interest is education, broadly; its method, comprehensive. Individual interests are aided only as the common interest is safeguarded."

The U. S. Supreme Court quoted approvingly the grounds for the Louisiana court decision, upholding the constitutionality of the statute: (a) the law did not provide for the purchase of books for sectarian schools; (b) by providing for free books for the children of the state the law was obviously enacted for the benefit of the children and the "resulting benefit of the State"; (c) the schools are not the beneficiaries of the statute; (d) the books furnished by the state are not sectarian books; (e) none, it is to be expected, would be adapted to religious instruction.

The state of Mississippi passed a law in 1941 providing for the free loan of textbooks to the pupils in all qualified elementary schools in the state. Suit was brought to prevent the state textbook board from extending this piece of legislation to pupils in private and parochial schools. The Supreme Court of Mississippi upheld the constitutionality of the measure in an opinion which is the clearest statement yet made of what is involved in a denial of the state's welfare benefits to all its children. "There is no requirement," said the Mississippi court, "that the church should be a liability to those of its citizens who are at the same time citizens of the state, and entitled to privileges and benefits as such."

The court agreed that the religion to which children of school age adhere is not subject to state control, but the children themselves are subject to its control. The decision stated further:

If the pupil may fulfil its duty to the state by attending a parochial school it is difficult to see why the state may not fulfil its duty to the pupil by encouraging it "by all suitable means." *The state is under duty to ignore the child's creed, but not its need.* It cannot control what one child may think, but it can and must do all it can to teach the child how to think. The state which allows the pupil to subscribe to any religious creed should not, because of his exercise of this right, proscribe him from benefits common to all.[20]

The tribunal scored the narrow construction contended for by the complainants, which would compel the pupil to surrender use of his books "when and because he elected to transfer from a public school to a qualified parochial school." This, the court said, would constitute "a denial of equal privileges on sectarian grounds."

One of the most heatedly debated applications of the child welfare doctrine is the use of public funds to transport children to parochial and other nonpublic schools. In fact, for some communities the school bus has become a symbol of strife and disunion. Catholic parents and taxpayers feel doubly aggrieved over this contention, because they consider bus transportation more than a legally approved welfare benefit. They look upon it as a fundamental safety measure which the state should unhesitatingly supply to all children.

It is a matter of fact that the reason the states came to assume responsibility for school transportation was precisely concern for the safety of the child. "Most school administrators," says a recent study by the U. S. Office of Education, "would concede that there is a very fundamental difference between pupil transportation and most of the other aspects of the school program. Transportation is primarily a service and is only incidentally related to the education of the child." This must be evidently the case, says the

[20] *Chance* v. *Mississippi State Textbook Board,* 200 So. 706 (1941). (Emphasis added.)

report, for "no school system would spend large amounts of money for the small educational benefits that might be derived during the period of transportation . . . [whose] fundamental purpose is to place the child at a location where certain educational opportunities are available. . . ."[21]

Safety was one of the primary reasons for convening the first national conference on school bus standards in 1939. Safety was the major reason for the enactment of the "school bus stop law" in most states. Currently, safety is the main reason for the movement for adequate standards and for training programs for school bus drivers.

In 1925–26 approximately 1.1 million youngsters rode the school buses, for which the tax tab was $35.6 million. In 1954–55 the cost of transporting 9.3 million pupils was $325 million. It has been estimated that 31 per cent of all public school pupils are carried to school at public expense. This accounts for an average of 4.5 pennies of each dollar in current school budgets, but in the budget of a suburban or rural school district the cost of transportation is considerably higher than the national average.

Constitutional or statutory authority to provide free transportation for pupils in nonpublic schools exists in twenty states—Alabama, Alaska, California, Colorado, Connecticut, Illinois, Indiana, Kansas, Kentucky, Louisiana, Maryland, Massachusetts, Michigan, New Hampshire, New Jersey, New Mexico, New York, Oregon, Rhode Island, and West Virginia. Though not provided for by law, some transportation is provided parochial school children in at least six other states. In sum, parochial school youngsters in twenty-six states with a combined population of some 90 millions—over one half the nation's total population—are riding to school in buses at public expense.

The state of Texas has a law under which half fare for transportation to school is given to all school children. This reduced fare transportation affects "all persons or corporations owning or operating street railways or motor buses in or upon the public streets of any city of not less than 12,000 inhabitants."

Similarly, in most cities reduced fares are made available to all school children on bus and trolley lines, whether these facilities

21 *Pupil Transportation Responsibilities and Services of State Departments of Education*, Misc. No. 27, p. 6.

are owned by the municipality or by a private corporation. In a number of states, where reductions for parochial school pupils have been challenged, the attorney general has interpreted existing public school free transportation laws so as to include them.

In those states where transportation is authorized for parochial school pupils but public school funds may be expended only for public school purposes, transportation is provided only along regular routes to and from public schools, or is financed through funds that have not been raised or levied for public school education. Indiana and Kentucky provide examples of both kinds of statutory authorization. In Montana nonpublic school children may ride the public school buses, provided parents or school pay a proportionate share of the cost of such transportation.

On the issue of free public transportation for parochial school children the state courts have been divided. California (1946), Kentucky (1945), Maryland (1938), Massachusetts (1955), and New Jersey (1945) courts have approved such measures; whereas, courts in Delaware (1938), Missouri (1953), New York (1938), Oklahoma (1941), South Dakota (1931), Washington (1943 and 1949), and Wisconsin (1923) have given negative decisions. However, in some of these latter decisions the precise point of dispute was not the transportation of parochial school students. The Missouri case concerned only the use of public school funds for parochial school children. In Wisconsin the question decided by the court was that a school district had gone beyond its statutory authority in contracting for the transportation of parochial school children after a school district reorganization. In the wake of the New York Supreme Court's 4-3 unfavorable ruling, the New York State Constitutional Convention of 1938, by a vote of 134-9, amended the basic education law to allow the transportation of children to and from any school in the state.

The 1945 Kentucky decision upholding the expenditure of public funds for transporting children to sectarian schools, provided that such funds were not regular school funds, is typical of other state court decisions. The State Supreme Court of Kentucky declared:

In this advanced and enlightened age, with all of the progress that has been made in the field of humane and social legislation, and with the hazards and dangers of the highway increased a thousandfold from what they formerly were, and with our compulsory school attendance laws applying to all children and being rigidly enforced, as they are, it cannot be said with any reason or consistency that tax legislation to provide our school children with safe transportation is not tax legislation for a public purpose.[22]

The New Jersey Supreme Court's decision was the first pupil-transportation case that reached the U. S. Supreme Court. There the court upheld the constitutionality of school bus transportation for parochial school students, comparing such facilities with fire and police protection offered to all schools indiscriminately. The court recognized that the New Jersey law did no more than implement the compulsory education law by providing "a general program to help parents get their children, regardless of their religion, safely and expeditiously to and from accredited schools." Briefs in support of the constitutionality of the New Jersey law (*Everson* case) were presented by the states of Illinois, Indiana, Louisiana, Massachusetts, Michigan, and New York.

The two critical points of the *Everson* decision—the state's concern for the safety of children in attending parochial schools and the universal operation of the compulsory education law—should be universally valid. Opponents of bus transportation as a welfare benefit argue that *Everson* settled only the federal question, i.e., such a law does not violate the First Amendment. This was the contention of the Supreme Court of the state of Washington in its 1949 decision, when for the second time this court declared unconstitutional a transportation law passed for the second time by the state legislature.

22 *Nichols* v. *Henry,* 191 SW 2d 930. The Kentucky Supreme Court added, "Neither can it be said that such legislation, or such taxation, is in aid of a church or of a private, sectarian or parochial school, nor that it is other than what it is designed and purports to be . . . legislation for the health and safety of our children, the future citizens of our State."

The Maryland Supreme Court, in giving its approval, stated: "The institution must be considered as aided only incidentally, the aid only being a by-product of proper legislative action" (*Board of Education* v. *Wheat,* 199 A 628).

The California Supreme Court, in its favorable decision, ruled: ". . . at best, transportation of parochial school students only resulted in an 'indirect' benefit to the private school" (*Bowker* v. *Baker,* 167 P 2d 256).

The pivotal point settled by the *Everson* case, however, is not the constitutionality of the specific New Jersey statute, but the solemn declaration by the highest legal court of the United States that *a state may constitutionally transport children to nonpublic schools—that a tax imposed for this purpose does not violate the so-called "wall of separation" between church and state.*

The appropriation of funds to directly reimburse parents for expenses incurred in sending children to a parochial school on a public conveyance and the fact that only Catholic parents were involved were the factors that led Justice Jackson to enter his separate dissenting opinion in *Everson*. Later, however, in his concurring opinion in the *McCollum* case, he said that if the resolution of the school board in the *Everson* case had been "for the protection of the safety, health or morals of youngsters it would not merely have been constitutional to grant it. It would have been unconstitutional to refuse it to any child merely because he was a Catholic."

That is the central question, which has yet to be squarely faced by the courts. It is not whether the extension of such "auxiliary services" to pupils in nonpublic schools is permitted by our fundamental laws, but whether our fundamental laws do not *require* such extension under the "equal protection of the laws," guaranteed by the federal Constitution.[23]

[23] The court recognized the right, but not the *duty*, to provide transportation. As George E. Reed has indicated: "Some advocates of free school bus transportation have failed to recognize this anomalous limitation in the *Everson* case, with the result that actions have been brought to force school boards to extend transportation service in the absence of essential enabling legislation. Uniformly, the courts have ruled adversely. . . ." "The School Bus Challenge," *The Catholic Lawyer*, Vol. 5, No. 2 (Spring 1959). For example, on May 25, 1959, the Maine Supreme Court unanimously agreed that neither the Maine nor the U. S. Constitution forbids free bus transportation to children attending nonpublic schools. However, the court, in a 4–2 split, ruled that state legislation was necessary before city officials could appropriate funds to transport nonpublic school pupils. The court affirmed that "we are satisfied that a properly worded enabling act . . . would meet Constitutional requirements."

CHAPTER 8

Attitudes and Proposals

Since the time of Archbishop Hughes of New York and the controversial 1840s, the Catholic position on education has remained substantially the same. There has always been insistence on these points: secular education must be integrated with religious education; a weekly catechism lesson in Sunday school is an inadequate substitute; attendance at public schools, because of a Protestant and secularist orientation, can prove spiritually harmful for Catholic children; ideally, Catholic children should be educated in Catholic schools.

From the side of Catholic parents these principles of the civil order have been maintained: parents have the paramount right to direct the education of their children; the free exercise of this right is contingent upon access to the practical means; the state taxes all citizens alike to form a common pool for the support of education but uses this money exclusively for a type of school which, for reasons of conscience, Catholic parents are unwilling to patronize; these parents, because of religious convictions, are forced to pay twice for the education of their children.

The rising costs of construction and teachers' salaries, along with additional responsibilities that the school is assuming, have steadily pushed skyward the nation's total school bill. The public school bill for 1958–59 was an estimated $14.4 billion—an increase of nearly 10 per cent over the preceding year. Officials of the National Education Association say the figure will be $20 billion in 1965 and around $30 billion by 1975.

A part of the increased cost of education is explained by new and improved services that the American school is expected to provide its pupils. For the elementary schools there are nurses, specialists in remedial reading, psychologists, experts in the latest forms of pupil testing and audio-visual techniques. For the high schools there are, in addition to these services, a widely diversified athletic program, domestic science, vocational training, and industrial arts programs. Closed TV circuits in the school, completely equipped home economics or "shop" wings, fleets of buses for the growing number of consolidated schools—these things do not come cheaply. Salaries of the clerical, maintenance, and supervisory staff of a large secondary school are a formidable item in the modern school budget. Meanwhile, in a less spectacular way the cost of Catholic schooling has been rising, owing in large part to the greater proportion of salaried lay teachers on faculties.

Young Catholic families in which there are three, four, or five school-age youngsters particularly feel the burden of supporting two educational systems. The Catholic laity and clergy are fully aware that direct basic support by the government to parochial schools is out of the question, for at least four reasons:

1. The U. S. Supreme Court would interpret such action as a contravention of the Federal Constitution.

2. Almost all state constitutions specifically rule out the support of sectarian schools.

3. Government support, especially federal, could readily bring such qualifications that the schools would lose their present independence.

4. Most of all, the rancor and strife set off by organized Catholic efforts to obtain such aid would poison community relations for years to come.

The admission, however, that direct basic governmental support is a present impossibility, or even an impossibility for several more generations, is not an abjuration of the Catholic claim to support in principle, for this is basically a question of civil rights. We shall elaborate on the point before putting a finish to this chapter.

But what do Catholics want *now*? Fundamentally, they want a sympathetic hearing for their case, public recognition of their problem, and help in working out an equitable solution. Though there is no authoritative expression of a single Catholic position

covering all these matters, there is a wide consensus among
clergy and laity that Catholic energies would be best spent on
achieving fuller distribution of educational items immediately related to the child benefit principle. The courts have indicated the
present legal dimensions of the principle. Leaving aside all reference to those items of basic institutional support, i.e., governmental grants for property sites, construction and maintenance of
buildings, salaries for the basic teaching, administrative, and
maintenance personnel, we can list other categories where action
could appropriately be taken.

Bus Transportation. Catholics judge that their children going
to parochial schools are entitled to the same transportation services that other children attending public schools receive. This
would mean that, within reason, the community would provide
home-to-school conveyance as is done for public school children.
Only a few states presently provide equal service.

Perhaps the most feasible solution to the transportation-of-
parochial-school-children problem in those states where it is
prevented by a real or imagined constitutional block, is to take
the State Department of Education out of the bus business. Since
operating a transportation system is primarily a noneducational
activity, it would fit more naturally into a more appropriate department. The "wall of separation" would appear far less formidable, if the State Highway Commission or the Department of
Highways or the Vehicle Licensing Department or the State
Motor Police were operating the buses rather than school districts
or state departments of education. After all, school districts
and departments of education have only received the franchise
through *delegation.* The state itself possesses the police power,
which it ordinarily delegates only to political subdivisions within
the state. There is nothing intrinsically educational about the
inspection of the tires on a school bus or the establishment of qualifications to drive a school bus. The following list gives some notion of how deeply involved our educational agencies are in the
bus business:[1]

[1] See *Pupil Transportation Responsibilities and Services of State Department of Education,* passim.

The State Department of Education:

in 34 states sets standards for school bus construction;

in 24 states sets standards for school bus drivers;

in 28 states sets standards under which handicapped children may be transported;

in 19 states assists in training programs for school bus maintenance personnel;

in 18 states operates school bus driver training schools;

in 15 states issues certificates of award for completion of school bus driver training;

in 4 states issues special school bus drivers' licenses;

in 7 states inspects and approves newly purchased school buses before they may be entered in service;

in 12 states makes periodic inspection of all school buses;

in 4 states approves licensing of buses before regular licensing agency issues registration tags;

in 2 states issues special registration tags to school buses.

The return of these noneducational activities to more appropriate jurisdiction would eliminate the legal (and emotional) argument against bus transportation for parochial school children; namely, that the use of funds collected by law for public schools would benefit sectarian education.

Textbooks. The practical value of free textbooks, at least as the program is presently administered, has been questioned by many Catholic educators. In states where parochial school children qualify for free textbooks, Catholic school officials have nothing to say about the preparation of the books, most of which they consider inadequate. The inevitable limitations under which the choice of a text for use in a common school in our pressure-group society must labor, render this benefit very limited, indeed. If the compass of the textbook program were expanded to include audio-visual aids, visiting special lecturers, traveling science exhibits, etc., Catholic interest would without doubt quicken.

Health Services. In some states children of all schools share equally in the federal and state funds appropriated for the lunch program, i.e., subsidized distribution of milk, orange juice, hot meals, etc. In most states, however, only federal funds are available for this program in parochial schools. Parochial school children, consequently, do not receive the full benefit of the program. Present practice regarding community health measures—vaccinations, medical and dental examinations, lung X rays, etc.—varies greatly, but probably most American communities find no constitutional scruple in extending these services to youngsters in a parochial school.

Testing and Guidance. When the National Defense Act of 1958 was finally passed by the Eighty-fifth Congress, there was widespread Catholic criticism of some provisions of the law.

In Title I, which states the philosophy of the Act, we read (1) that the security of the nation requires the fullest development of the mental resources and technical skills of its young men and women; (2) that we must increase our efforts to identify and educate more of the talent of the nation; (3) that no student of ability should be denied an opportunity for higher education because of financial need. It would be entirely reasonable to expect, then, that the benefits of this Act would apply indiscriminately to all students and all institutions. This is not the case.

In Title II there is provision for the cancellation of up to one half of any loan, plus interest, at a yearly rate of 10 per cent for college students who will enter full-time teaching in a *public* elementary or secondary school. No "forgiveness" of debt is granted to interest future teachers in nonpublic schools, where the pressures and the needs are just as great.

According to the terms of Title III, outright grants go to states for the acquisition of laboratory or other special equipment for instruction in science, mathematics, and modern foreign languages in *public* schools. Nonprofit, nonpublic schools may borrow money from the government for these same purposes. Under the same title there is provision for a grant to states for the expansion or improvement of supervisory services in the fields of mathematics, science, and foreign languages—but exclusively in *public* elementary and secondary schools or junior colleges.

Title V makes grants to assist *public* secondary schools in their counseling and guidance programs. (But what happens to the program in Rhode Island, for instance, where 31 per cent of the elementary and secondary school population is enrolled in parochial schools?) Those teachers who are preparing to work in *public* schools may, according to this title, while attending counseling institutes, receive a $75 weekly stipend for expenses, but other teachers receive nothing. Title VI contains an identical discriminatory clause, which works against those who attend government-sponsored centers for the preparation of foreign language teachers but do not plan to teach in *public* schools.

The 1958 National Defense Education Act does not distinguish between public and private institutions of higher learning, but it clearly does on the secondary and elementary school level. This piece of legislation, despite its many excellent provisions, pinpoints the Catholic grievance. The Act is projected for the defense of the American people; it offers support for the improved training of the nation's school population. Yet simply because they are in religiously oriented schools, Catholic students and teachers are accorded second-class treatment for fear of non-Catholic protest that the benefits of the Act might incidentally benefit Catholic institutions. Attempts were made in the Eighty-sixth Congress to temper some of the more glaring inequalities of the 1958 Act. But the question remains unanswered: During these years, when the nation cannot afford to leave any talent undeveloped, wherever available, have not Catholics the right to expect that government-supported programs in counseling, testing, and guidance will include their children in parochial schools? If the federal government in the interests of national defense and world leadership is going to help local communities to identify, guide, and subsidize student talent, it must do so indiscriminately. Where local prejudice or state constitutions make this impossible, the federal government should establish testing centers or language laboratories or science institutes independent of the public schools and accessible to all students.

Exceptional Children. Thirteen of every one hundred children of school age are classified today as "exceptional." This is an umbrellalike term that covers all students for whom extraordinary facilities must be provided by the school. There are 5 million exceptional children in the nation, and about 1.5 million are Catholic youngsters. The extra expense involved in providing adequately for these children has been beyond the financial ability of most Catholic school systems. Only in a few of the larger dioceses have programs been established to make Catholic education available for the physically incapacitated or mentally handicapped.

At present there is practically no provision in Catholic secondary schools for educable mentally retarded pupils, that is, those children with a 50–75 I.Q. but capable of slow learning. Even the large central Catholic high schools in most areas are presently forced to require entrance examinations or proof of academic achievement as a prerequisite for admission to their already overcrowded classrooms. The charge sometimes leveled at Catholic schools, particularly secondary schools, that they cater only to the "cream of the crop" has this much basis in fact: dearth of specially trained personnel and lack of facilities make it impossible for most Catholic schools to open their doors to certain less endowed youngsters.

Were there community support available to Catholic school systems for such programs, the situation would rapidly change, and there would be no grounds for the claim that Catholic schools make of the public schools "dumping grounds" for the less gifted and "problem" children. The freedom of choice in education for the Catholic parent of an exceptional child exists only if he has the means to place his son or daughter in one of the few institutional schools operated by a sisterhood. Yet how often these children are the very ones who most need the tender care and love that is often best given in religious surroundings. These "special" cases illuminate the rich depths of the Catholic philosophy of education which sees the worth of the blighted mind or the crippled little body and can lovingly communicate to it the values of the supernatural—the goal of eternity and the mystery of suffering.

Tax Credits. Various tax credit plans or educational voucher plans to pay the tuition and fees of college and graduate students have been proposed. In fact, a number of bills embodying some form of tax credit plan have been introduced in recent years into the legislatures of several states and into the Congress. For example, several of the score or more of tax credit bills that were introduced into the Eighty-fifth Congress provided that 30 per cent of the money paid in tuition or fees to public or private institutions of higher learning could be applied as a tax credit against federal income-tax assessment. In practice this would mean that a family which pays $500 in tuition and school fees would be able to deduct $150 from the federal income tax. The suggestion of Father Virgil C. Blum, S.J., a professor of political science at Marquette University, that pupils in elementary and secondary schools should be made the beneficiaries of similar plans is being widely discussed.

The tax credit plan for college students, both in public and nonpublic institutions, has the support of a number of national educational organizations, including the Association of American Colleges, the Association of State Universities, the American Council on Education, and the American Alumni Council. The President's Committee on Education Beyond the High Schools has made the recommendation that "the Federal revenue laws be revised . . . in ways which will permit deductions or credits on income tax returns by students, their parents or others who contribute to meeting the expenditures necessarily incurred in obtaining formal education beyond high school. . . ."[2]

As Father Blum has painstakingly pointed out in his book, *Freedom of Choice in Education,*

> The certificate or tax credit plan is in principle the same as the plans the Federal Government adopted to enable veterans, war orphans, and the pages of Congress to get an education at the school of their choice. The direct subsidy principle, incorporating the principle of freedom of choice, was adopted, in one form or another, in the Servicemen's Readjustment Act of 1944, the Veterans' Readjustment Act of 1952, the War Orphans' Educational Assistance Act of 1956, and in the educational provisions of the Legislative Reorganization Act of 1946 for the education of the pages of Congress.[3]

[2] *Second Report to the President. The President's Committee on Education Beyond the High School* (July 1957), p. 11.
[3] (New York: Macmillan, 1958), p. 30.

Non-Catholic opposition to the claims just presented in the name of the school child derives, in the main, from two concerns. Some Protestants and other non-Catholics fear that granting even a few incidental benefits to Catholic schools will serve to strengthen what they consider the growing power of the Catholic Church in American society. Much of this fear is—in Catholic eyes —unreasonable, inherited prejudice. In any event, it exists and must be taken into account.

An even larger group of Americans bases its opposition on the fear that whatever favors the growth of private education serves to weaken public education—that any government step facilitating the expansion of parochial schools redounds to the harm of public schools. It is not wise for Catholics to dismiss this position impatiently, or to categorize all those who hold it as bigoted, spiteful, or godless. If Catholic schools were to get basic support, these people are convinced, a profusion of other church schools will spring up in a chain reaction that could ultimately destroy our traditional public school system. Those who share this opinion profess to see a nightmare, in which dozens of church- or sectarian-sponsored schools with state subsidy will fragmentize American education.

How, these objectors ask, could a town of 5,000 inhabitants support ten or twelve sectarian schools, each competing for community support? In place of a single strong public school for all children, the town would end up dividing its children and its money among a dozen mediocre schools. In the parochialism, bickering, and rivalry that would ensue, what would happen to civic unity and harmony? Moreover, the argument continues, consider the consequences of allowing some of the hundreds of splinter denominations to get into education. What would prevent an enterprising storefront minister with 2,000 signatures from members of his Thirty-third Church of Heavenly Holiness from obtaining government support to found a school too? These are trump arguments brought out to prove the impracticality of granting any state support to Catholic parochial schools.

Oddly enough, those who propose such difficulties never seem to consider the manner in which the same situation is handled in any one of a score of other countries that legally subsidize independent religious schools, and whose citizens count themselves lovers of freedom and democracy as much as do Americans.[4] Separate school systems, subsidized in whole or in part by the government, under the auspices of the major church groups are actually operating with success in many countries—England, Ireland, Scotland, Belgium, Holland, India, Canada, et al. After all, there are reasonable requirements and standards that the state can lay down to avoid exactly the kind of educational chaos and dissipation of school resources these objectors fear. Only religious groups that can guarantee a continuing sufficiency of prospective pupils may qualify for a school charter and assistance. Some countries, like Great Britain, supply only a portion of the funds needed to establish and operate the school. The sponsoring group must still truly support its school. The state prescribes the general curriculum, licenses teachers, and conducts the examinations for promotion for these schools, just as for all others.

What is the present status of church-sponsored education in the United States? Eight out of some 250 religious groups, other than the Catholic Church, have established school systems of any size, which in the aggregate enroll about 500,000 pupils. Three of these are among the 17 religious bodies that have a membership of a million or more—the Lutheran Church-Missouri Synod, the Protestant Episcopal Church, and the Jewish congregations. The five other denominations with school systems are Evangelical Lutheran Joint Synod of Wisconsin and other states, Seventh-Day Adventists, Mennonite Church (including Amish), Society of Friends, and the Christian Reformed Church. The National Association of Christian Churches also lists some 150 schools under the sponsorship of local churches of different denominations. Some of these local churches operate schools, even though their national denominations do not promote educational programs.[5]

The evangelical Protestant groups including the Baptists (20 million) and the Methodists (12 million) have never known the tradition of church schools. Since these groups represent the bulk of the membership in the American Protestant churches, there is

---

[4] The most recent compilation of facts and statistics can be found in *Public Funds for Private Schools in a Democracy: Theory and Practice in Fifty-one Countries*, Benigno Benabarre (Manila, P.I.: M.C.S. Enterprises, 1958).

[5] These figures are quoted from *Information Service*, publication of the Bureau of Research and Survey, National Council of the Churches of Christ in the U.S.A., January 3, 1959.

small likelihood that they would undertake parochial school systems similar to those of the Catholic Church.

Back of the intransigence of some people to accept even the court-approved general welfare benefits for parochial school children is a critical question: Where does the principle of child welfare logically stop? If this principle can be invoked to provide free bus transportation and free textbooks for parochial school children, why can't it be used to justify every other expense connected with schooling? What is to prevent the state from providing cafeterias, clinics, swimming pools, football stadiums, and gymnasiums for parochial schools—always, of course, with a view to benefiting the child's health? As one dissenting Supreme Court justice in the *Everson* case argued: "Every step in the educational process is, presumably, for the benefit of the child," and consequently, if the argument for child welfare is sound, "it is within the discretion of the legislature, free of constitutional restraint, to provide for practically the entire cost of education in private and parochial as well as in public schools."

In fact, the federal department which deals with educational affairs calls itself the Department of Health, Education and Welfare, indicating the natural closeness of the three ideas and that education itself is a welfare benefit. It is not so much today's buses and lunches but tomorrow's salaries, buildings, and fully subsidized parochial school system that rouses non-Catholic opposition. These people ask: Are there any limitations to the child welfare concept other than what the Catholic community feels it can successfully push for? What guarantee is there that Catholic leadership will confine its demands on the public purse to the so-called "child welfare benefits"? Though this loaded question seems highly unreasonable to anyone who understands the Catholic position, it must be dealt with.

The first answer that comes to mind is the simple retort: Why should there be any guarantee? Catholics do not look upon the claim to share in general welfare benefits—including education itself—as a raid on the public treasury but as an issue to be argued in the civic forum because it concerns *civil* rights. But if such a guarantee or "treaty of limitations" were proper, who should make it, and upon whom would it be binding? Does the matter call for a papal concordat or a solemn proclamation by the American bishops? Non-Catholics tend to think only of the Catholic hierarchy with reference to the school problem, as if Catholic citizen-parents were somehow outside of it all. Catholics themselves often furnish the grounds for this misunderstanding by their failure to make it clear that they are acting—and are expected to act—independently in the civic forum.

It is Catholic belief that Christ entrusted to the Apostles and their episcopal successors the office of teaching His revelation. The bishops, accordingly, have a pastoral mandate which all Catholics acknowledge. In consequence of their teaching office the bishops and their delegates have taken the lead in raising funds to build, staff, and maintain church schools in which both religious and secular education take place. The immediate episcopal concern is the religious aspect of education, but this inevitably puts the bishops in the center of most school questions. Moreover, according to civil law the control of Catholic parochial school property is legally vested in the bishop as head of the diocesan corporation, and according to canon law the bishop alone has the right to establish parochial or diocesan schools. Even an exempt religious order or a group of laymen who may wish to start a school must have the bishop's approval in order to designate their school as "Catholic." The lay-clerical relationship in religious affairs, as well as the central position of the bishop in civil and canon law, has unfortunately resulted in an underemphasis on the collaborative and directive role of the Catholic laity in school matters.[6]

The Catholic laity have only in recent years begun to work closely in significant numbers with the bishops and pastors, in other than the fund-raising aspects of Catholic education. In an increasing number of parishes, parents are already playing an important advisory role in parochial school affairs. Far-seeing pastors are relying more and more upon the leadership of their parishioners in meeting school problems and planning policy. In 1958 the diocesan school superintendents of the six dioceses of Ohio recommended to their respective bishops that qualified lay Catholics

---

[6] "We willingly encourage whatever facilitates and makes possible a closer collaboration between school and family. . . . The latter must not and, indeed, cannot abdicate its directive function; collaboration is natural and necessary" (Pius XII, *Acta Apostolicae Sedis*, January 5, 1954).

be invited to serve on the diocesan school boards, a measure which is gradually being implemented. This innovation recalls that much overlooked decree of the Third Plenary Council of Baltimore which says: "Let laymen also be given, in regard to the schools, certain rights and privileges to be determined by diocesan statutes. . . ."

Modern preoccupation with civil rights has made everyone more aware of rights in education. The question of civil rights in education is more the province of parents than of the clergy. As a matter of fact, civil society does not directly recognize the ecclesiastical nature of church schools; it views them as nonprofit *private* educational corporations with ecclesiastical trustees, which serve a group of its citizens. The claims in distributive justice for parochial school children to participate in the state's welfare benefits are made, then, not for the school in the name of the ecclesiastical trustees, but for the school child in the name of the citizen-parents. Theoretically, if every Catholic bishop in the United States stated his refusal to accept direct basic subsidy for parochial schools, this would not affect the freedom of citizen-parents to ask for full government support for the education of their children. In other words, when a bishop adopts policies for church schools in his diocese he does not in the least intend to compromise, waive, or ignore the civil rights of American citizens who, as Catholics, happen to be his religious subjects. If the school problem is essentially one of civil rights it will have to be settled eventually on that level. Citizen must persuade citizen in the forum of civic affairs. No solution will come through an exchange of "summit" statements between the National Council of Churches of Christ and the National Catholic Welfare Conference.

Nonetheless, because the bishops have the pastoral and legal control of Catholic parochial and diocesan schools, and because the laity respect the opinions of their bishops, what the hierarchy has to say about government aid to education is important. What have the American Catholic bishops said, individually and collectively, on the issue? First, it should be recalled from an earlier chapter that there are 140 dioceses in the country, that each diocese is independent of the others, and that each diocesan school system is an independent unit. A formal statement of school policy by one bishop will not be binding, therefore, except in his own diocese.

In 1949 during the controversy over the Barden bill—the first general federal-aid measure to receive serious Congressional consideration after World War II—several Catholic bishops publicly stated their positions. For example, the Archbishop of New York, Francis Cardinal Spellman, said: "We are not asking for general public support of religious schools." He pointed out that in the state of New York, as in practically every other state, constitutional provisions barred the use of public funds for the support of sectarian schools, and that such was also the interpretation of the Federal Constitution by the U. S. Supreme Court. "Under the Constitution," he said, "we do not ask nor can we expect public funds to pay for the construction or repair of parochial school buildings, or for the support of teachers or for other maintenance costs." Cardinal Spellman emphasized, however, that the subject of the 1949 controversy was not basic institutional support. He indicated the incidental expenses involved in education—transportation, nonreligious textbooks, and health aids—which were.[7]

Cardinal Spellman's position and his distinction between basic subsidy to the school and auxiliary services for the school child have been seconded in public statements by other bishops. The administrative board of bishops of the National Catholic Welfare Conference whose annual statements reflect, as much as any public statements can, the official policy of the American hierarchy, have stated the same position.

One consideration that leads some Catholic bishops to eye state support for church schools with suspicion has been stated by Richard Cardinal Cushing, Archbishop of Boston. Speaking of government aid, he said: "I would absolutely refuse the offer, for I cannot see how any Government or State would build schools, without expecting to control them in whole or in part. We are not looking to any Government for any assistance in building our system of education."[8] There are certainly ample historical grounds for this mistrust. Once church schools are liable to the detailed accounting, supervision, and inspection which the state normally exacts as the price of its subsidy, the control of education can eas-

[7] New York *Times*, August 6, 1949.
[8] Speech, December 8, 1955.

ily slip into the hands of the state, or at least can be dominated by a state philosophy of education. Such an eventuality might still appear remote in America, but for anyone conversant with the history of education in Europe during the last century, or of the precarious *modus vivendi* of Catholic schools in certain countries today, the sincerity of this concern should be apparent.

The following is a reasonable summary of the points of policy representing the views of the two societies that have the principal stake in Catholic education—the family, through the parents, and the Church, through the bishops and pastors.

1. The parents of children in parochial schools have always been free as citizens and voters to work for legal measures that would alleviate the double burden of school taxation they presently bear. They have the right to expect that the federal and state governments will assist them in every way legally possible to finance the education of their children in schools of parental choice.

2. These parents insist that their children have every right to share in all of the state's general welfare benefits, and in any special legislation designed to develop academic and scientific leadership for the nation. General welfare legislation includes at least the specific benefits of bus transportation, nonreligious textbooks, and health services, all of which have been upheld in principle by the American courts. An additional "parent-benefit" measure, that might later be provided by law, would be some form of income-tax adjustment which would allow a deduction for money expended on tuition and fees.

3. Conceivably, groups of Catholic parents could organize their own private school corporations, receive ecclesiastical recognition, and ask the government for direct subsidies to build, staff, and maintain these schools—as is done in many countries today.

4. For their part, the bishops have not asked, and have indicated that they will not ask, for basic institutional subsidy for parochial schools. They have specified that their understanding of basic support includes public grants for buildings, maintenance, and ordinary salaries.

5. This episcopal policy is based on a consideration of constitutional barriers, implications of government control, and the present climate of public opinion.[9] It is a *policy*, therefore, adopted in view of what the bishops deem the best interests of the Church and the nation. The bishops of 2060 might well be influenced by the conditions of that year to adopt another policy. They would no more be bound by a policy set by the bishops of 1960 than were these latter prelates bound by the school policy of the bishops of 1860.

6. Any changes in the laws relating to the degree of support for nonpublic schools will take place in the democratic manner, through a change in public policy. This will occur when—and if —the American people generally accept the justice of the case of the Catholic parent. The prevailing consensus among Catholic clerical and lay leaders is, however, that for many years to come it would be futile to press for full direct support for parochial school education.

In the aftermath of the *McCollum* decision, which in effect put the state on the side of godless education, the Catholic bishops in their annual statement for 1948 voiced their deep conviction that "for the sake of both good citizenship and religion there should be a reaffirmation of our original American tradition of free cooperation between Government and religious bodies—cooperation involving no special privilege to any group and no restriction on the religious liberty of any citizen."[10]

In the unbroken tradition of Carroll, Spalding, Ireland, Gibbons, and other distinguished leaders of the American hierarchy, the bishops then repeated the principle that has guided the American Catholic Church since the birth of the United States: "We solemnly disclaim any intent or desire to alter this prudent and fair American policy in dealing with the delicate problems that

[9] In a public address Bishop Matthew F. Brady of Manchester, N.H., then chairman of the Education Department of the N.C.W.C., referred to the question of some support for parochial schools in the name of parental rights. "There is not the slightest possibility of such a solution," he said, "in the present state of American public opinion." Before a satisfactory solution can be found, "justice and the framework of our Constitution must be more carefully scrutinized, unreasoned fears dissipated, a spirit of tolerance and fairness fostered, a humble approach made in confidence of God's guidance. . . ." (See *America*, May 26, 1956.)

[10] "The Christian in Action," annual statement of the hierarchy, November 20, 1948 (reprinted in full in *The Catholic Mind*, January 1949).

have their source in the divided religious allegiance of our citizens."[11]

The Church-state controversy over support for the schools reached a climax with the *Everson* decision in which the U. S. Supreme Court approved New Jersey's use of public funds for the transportation of parochial school children. The reckless charge was widely circulated that Catholics now felt free to open an all-out campaign to destroy the constitutional principle of Church-state separation. For whatever good it might have in re-assuring sincere non-Catholics, the late Archbishop John T. Mc-Nicholas of Cincinnati, speaking with his authority as chairman of the Administrative Board of the American Bishops National Catholic Welfare Conference, stated:

> No group in America is seeking union of Church and state; and least of all are Catholics. We deny absolutely and without any qualification that the Catholic Bishops of the United States are seeking a union of Church and state by any endeavors what-soever, either proximate or remote. If tomorrow Catholics con-stituted a majority in our country, they would not seek a union of Church and state. They would then, as now, uphold the Con-stitution and all its Amendments, recognizing the moral obliga-tion imposed on all Catholics to observe the Constitution and its Amendments.[12]

Few if any Catholic dioceses have enough parochial school classrooms to accommodate every Catholic child of elementary and secondary school age. The existing Catholic schools in some smaller dioceses provide a seat for every child, but the shift to the suburbs and the scattered Catholic population in rural sections of

[11] Ibid.

[12] New York *Times,* January 26, 1948; also quoted in Stokes, II, 715. This was the formal reply of Archbishop McNicholas to the public manifesto of a group called "Protestants and Other Americans United for the Separation of Church and State," issued January 12, 1948. The prelate scored two solid points which should be repeated from time to time. He wrote: "The signers of the manifesto assume that their attempt to have the Supreme Court reverse its decision is a patriotic virtue, but that it is criminal for others to seek an interpretation of an Amendment to the Constitution.

"The manifesto also stigmatizes as unwarranted pressure the action of the Catholic hierarchy in presenting its views on proposed Federal legislation. At the same time, the signers of the manifesto propose to do that very thing, by influencing legislatures, the judiciary and executives."

these same dioceses mean that many children cannot be taken care of. What does the Church do for her children in public schools, for all those who with or without good reason are not in church schools?

Unfortunately, until recent years the organizational energy of the American Church seemed to have been taken up with the favored half of the child population that was in the Catholic school, leaving the other half to feel, as the parent of one of these left-outs put it, "that at best they are victims of an unfortunate geographical location."

More and more pastors are recognizing that the neglect of the "unhoused" half results in dividing a parish. There are those parishioners who have gone through Catholic schools, and these people generally end up as pillars of the parish. Then there are the others who are not closely identified with the religious and social life of the parish. Even more unfortunate is the division among the children. There are the children in the parish school who sing in the parish choirs, perform the altar service, wear the parochial school emblem, and are closely identified with the parish. Then there are the children in the public schools who somehow are looked upon as never quite belonging, and who as adults will gravitate toward the fringes of the parish, and generally fall into a kind of second-class citizenship in the Church.

Since the post-World War II population boom, however, new and more effective methods of reaching Catholic children in public schools have been developed.[13] The most important factor here undoubtedly is the growth of the Confraternity of Christian Doctrine, or the C.C.D. This is a co-ordinated program under diocesan direction which prepares lay and religious part-time teachers for teaching religion to Catholic youth in public schools. The ideal envisioned here goes much beyond the one-hour, one-day-a-week released-time program—though in cases this may be the program's starting point—whose role in the educational process Justice Frankfurter likened to the enforced weekly piano lesson. Thousands of parishes have now organized a volunteer corps of teachers, teaching assistants, and home visitors who impart religious instruction, plan religious and social activities for the

[13] A splendid selection of essays on religious education is contained in *Shaping the Christian Message*, ed. Gerard S. Sloyan (New York: Macmillan, 1958).

children, and, perhaps most valuable of all, enfold these young-sters into the normal life of the parish.

It is becoming a standard practice in parishes to bring together all the children—those in the public schools as well as those in the parochial school—for regular religious occasions. These young people sit together at the children's Mass on Sunday, they make their First Communion and Confirmation together, they join, whenever possible, in the choir and altar-boy service of the church. From their school years on, these youngsters are given a full sense of belonging.

Parents of children in public schools, however, have a special responsibility for seeing that their children receive a full moral and religious education. This means that parents are expected to interest themselves in what goes on within the school. This entails as a minimum that parents make a reasonable acquaintance with the teaching methods and textbooks used in the school. It can happen that high school texts in biology or social studies will contain seriously offensive matter, e.g., relating to sex education, atheistic evolution, naturalistic theories of the origin of religion, etc., to which parents in conscience must object. Needless to say, knowledge and supervision of the child's extracurricular and social activities is also part of parental responsibility.

Moreover, Catholic parents of children in public schools are gravely obliged to see that their children fully participate in the religious instruction program and related C.C.D. activities. They should insist that the youngster form regular habits of receiving the sacraments and attending Mass and following the observances of the liturgical year.

Parents of Catholic children in the public schools appreciate full well the impossibility of regular sectarian religious instruction within them. Yet these parents have every right to resent and to oppose the constant efforts of some groups of citizens to eliminate every trace of religion from the public schools. These are the people in the forefront of every campaign to keep references to God and belief in God out of policy statements on moral and spiritual values which try to spell out the relevance of religion to education. Granted that such statements are not a wonder-recipe for the moral ills of society or proof of the moral and spiritual well-being of education, there are sound reasons why such declarations should be part of community policy on public education.

First of all, these statements help to ensure that our children do not grow up as religious illiterates. If the public schools are forced by minority pressure to ignore religion in education, they cannot give our young citizens a proper appreciation of the historical orientation of their country. Nor is this a matter of "indoctrination." It is education. An educated person should be familiar with his heritage, and for an American this means in the main the culture of the West. Interwoven with the history, literature, and arts of Western civilization is the great Judeo-Christian tradition. To prune out or to pass lightly over the religious aspects of our heritage for fear of offending a minority is a strange mutilation of the education process. It would be as logical to stop concentrating on the classics of the English language in a literature class for fear of giving offense to Americans of Asiatic origin.

Moreover, formal policy statements on values assist in the creation of that hardy moral climate which must exist if impressionable young minds are to absorb ethical and spiritual values. Where there is frank official acknowledgement of belief in the God of our fathers and His eternal law, a public school teacher need not stand tongue-tied, afraid of reprisal, when a disciplinary situation or class matter naturally calls for a discussion of moral obligation and she relates these to religious values and sanctions. Diversity of religious backgrounds among her pupils requires on the teacher's part tact, prudence, and understanding—not just silence.

Religion has always been vitally associated with the moral and spiritual ideals of mankind. No people has ever based its mores solely on an ethic of pure reason. Yet to exclude mention of God's Ten Commandments, for example, as a motive for proper behavior is silently to encourage our school children to mere natural morality. A Catholic wants none of that for his child. He agrees in principle with Washington's farewell warning to his countrymen:

And let us with caution indulge the supposition that morality can be maintained without religion. Whatever may be conceded to the influence of refined education on minds of peculiar structure, reason and experience both forbid us to expect that national morality can prevail in exclusion of religious principle.

The principal reason for formal statements on values, however, is the need to throw up a barrier against the increasing pressure of those minorities who seek to completely secularize the public schools. In the face of the diversity of our religious loyalties the problem of preparing a statement of values which will be thoroughly acceptable to all is an obviously insoluble one. Nevertheless, it is a fact that, despite wide differences in belief, most Americans still take a view of life and the universe which is based on the reality of God. The public school must somehow preserve and foster our tradition of belief while protecting the rights of any families whose religious philosophy is not based on belief in a personal God.

Despite their intrinsic shortcomings, statements on values are important and needed, even if only for their symbolic value. Certain small groups are not content when proposed policy statements on moral and spiritual values are broadly enough written to ensure respect for their own dissent. In the name of separation of church and state, or of equal protection in law, they insist that these statements respect only their dissent. To yield to such importuning, either by abandonment of policy statements or by so diluting them that they become meaningless, is to uproot the common school from the American tradition and to flout the reasonable desire of the overwhelming majority of American citizens.

Community harmony in some of the large metropolitan areas has been increasingly upset in recent years by another issue: the disputes over pageants and displays of religious significance in the public schools. These quarrels occur regularly during preparation for the Christmas and Easter seasons. It is with sorrow and chagrin that Catholic parents watch the steady obliteration of the traditional religious symbols of these holy seasons from the public schools.

What should be the attitude of Catholics when confronted with these situations? The different religious composition of American communities makes it impossible to invoke a blanket procedural norm, valid in detail, for the entire country. What takes place in one school may be extremely ill-advised in a school elsewhere. Generally speaking, however, is the public school under obligation to renounce all traditional symbols or observances in order to placate a few articulate objectors? Hardly, for this would, in effect, be to canonize a tenet of the secularist creed. However, majority wishes must always be balanced against the liberty and protection of the individual dissenting conscience. At the same time, an individual's right should not be allowed to neutralize reasonable majority action. Moreover, no child should be under compulsion to participate in school activities that run counter to his family's religious allegiance. Catholics have themselves suffered enough in American history to be able to appreciate the difficulties of a minority religious position.

In this context, perhaps a small word of caution is not out of place. The campaign to "Put Christ Back in Christmas" should not turn into an ugly display of group power. Christian parent groups should be cautious about pressing for the introduction of religious pageants and displays, where they have hitherto been unknown. Fair consideration must always be given to the legitimate objections and religious susceptibilities of dissenters.

Increased pains should be taken by Catholics to correct any impression that their interests in the public schools are exclusively negative or even sectarian. One half or more of the Catholic children of elementary and secondary school age are enrolled in public schools. If there were not a single Catholic child in them, Catholics would still have a serious obligation to concern themselves with the well-being of the public schools. If membership in the Catholic Church is not incompatible with a full sharing in civic and community life, neither is patronage of a parochial school a barrier to a Catholic's assumption of civic responsibility for public education. Many years ago when Father Paul L. Blakely, S.J., for his thirty-five years on the staff of *America* an intrepid champion of parents' rights in education, wrote that famous line, "Our first duty to the public school is not to pay taxes for its maintenance,"[14] he created a stir whose echoes are still occasionally heard. Father Blakely, with all due respect, was wrong. Let it be recalled, however, that those lines were written while the antireligious influence of the progressivist movement was at its height and bade fair to capture public education. Father Blakely struck so many solid blows for worthy social causes that he can readily be forgiven his

[14] *May an American Oppose the Public School?* (America Press pamphlet, 1937).

unfortunate statement on the Catholic duty toward the public school.

There is nothing in Catholic dogma or belief, however, that makes a virtue out of shirking the responsibilities of citizenship. Catholic citizens have as grave an obligation toward the common welfare of the nation as has anyone else, and the concept of the common welfare today includes publicly supported education. Because Catholics generally prefer to send their youngsters to parochial rather than to public schools, they are not, therefore, absolved from the civic obligation of moral and material support of the public schools. "It would be a dereliction of duty and an offense against both justice and charity," stated Archbishop Karl J. Alter of Cincinnati, "if it were to be assumed by representatives of church-related or private schools that their own interests could prosper at the expense of public school interests. No responsible Catholic authority has ever advocated any such attitude."[15]

During a recent election when bond issues for public schools were on the ballot for approval, bishops and Catholic school leaders in a score of cities issued public statements urging in the strongest terms that Catholic voters recognize their civic duty to vote for needed improvements in the local public school systems.[16] Increasingly in recent years state and national Catholic organizations of laymen and laywomen have adopted resolutions in support of the public schools. Cardinals, bishops, pastors, and lay leaders have continually urged in sermons, public addresses, and policy statements that Catholics join with their fellow citizens and provide for strong public schools. Yet, Catholics are still charged with opposing public schools, turning down school bond issues, and refusing to support public education.

When a Catholic shows sufficient interest in public schools to announce his candidacy for a place on the local school board, his motives immediately come under suspicion. All the more is this true if his own children are attending a parochial school, for many non-Catholics feel that this disqualifies him for such an office.

If a Catholic member of the U. S. Chamber of Commerce or

[15] "A National Educational Policy as Seen from a Catholic Viewpoint," an address given in Cincinnati, April 10, 1956.

[16] Here is a selection: Davenport, Iowa; Steubenville, Ohio; Seattle, Wash.; Peoria, Ill.; Rochester, N.Y.; St. Louis, Mo.; St. Paul, Minn.; Los Angeles, Calif.; Flint, Mich.

National Association of Manufacturers joins in any criticism of public school education, there are non-Catholics who decide this must be attributable to his Catholic anti-public school prejudices. This extreme sensitivity over Catholic criticism of public education—granted that there are cases of exaggerated or tactless criticism by Catholics—is based on the assumption that those who do not patronize the public school have no right to criticize it. This assumption passes over the fact that Catholics, as citizens, share the general concern in the welfare of the country, and the fact that they have as much right to make their views heard on matters of public interest—including the *public* schools—as has anyone else.

However, Catholic support of public schools does not mean an uncritical acceptance of every proposition for federal aid that happens to be proposed. Prescinding completely from the presence on the educational scene of nonpublic schools, a citizen and taxpayer has every right to examine on their merits all proposals for financing public school education. For example, he might find serious shortcomings in the kind of indiscriminate federal-aid legislation proposed in the Murray-Metcalf Bill of the Eighty-sixth Congress. He might judge that the pattern of school support and control should remain on the local level, or that federal aid would serve as a substitute for sluggish local effort, or that federal funds would be used to perpetuate segregated school systems. His opposition to federal aid does not imply opposition to public schools, nor would it be based on his loyalty to nonpublic school education.

On the other hand, it is understandably true that the financial burden of supporting a parochial school attended by their children can make a Catholic family less than enthusiastic over voting for even necessary increases for the public school budget. Young families of limited income find small solace in theories, when a practical decision must be made between pledging money to build a parochial school (which their youngsters will attend) or voting a property tax increase to put up a new public high school (which their children will not attend). It is in these situations that a Catholic parent and taxpayer feels that he is receiving less than equal justice under the law. Without his vote the public school bond issue cannot pass. Without his pledge the parochial school cannot be built. His loyalties and his pocketbook are pulled in two directions. Yet he did not create the dilemma: he is only its victim. He may be excused, though, if he sometimes wonders aloud why he should not be free to use at least a part of his school tax money for the kind of schooling he wants for his children. He also may be excused for his resentment, after he has loyally voted for the new public high school and fully assumed his share of support for public schooling, to find that most of his non-Catholic neighbors are totally unconcerned about his problem.

And yet there are encouraging signs that perceptive leaders in American society, and in public education particularly, are aware of the necessity and desirability of mutual understanding between public and nonpublic education. Dr. William G. Carr, executive secretary of the National Education Association, has offered suggestions for avoiding some of the acrimony that has in the past marked relations between the two systems and has made an effective partnership impossible.

He suggests that the leadership of the private schools make its position clear on the following points:[17]

1. That the public schools are necessary and respected institutions in these United States and that concern for their improvement and support is a general public responsibility of each citizen.

2. That such terms as "secular" and "pragmatic" as applied to education be restored to their normal descriptive purposes, and that the use of these words as vehicles of abuse and opprobrium be discontinued.

3. That, in so far as schools of any kind are responsible for the imperfections of our society and for evil behavior in general, that responsibility is shared by all schools, unless it can be shown that the graduates of private schools or of public schools are substantially more free of the particular faults than other persons.

4. That when school people disagree—as they surely will—on some of the basic issues of human life as well as of educational policy and political theory, they endeavor to persuade rather than to wound.

[17] Quoted in "Public and Private Schools Talk It Out," *America*, May 26, 1956.

In offering to private school leaders these "self-denying ordinances," Dr. Carr immediately added that spokesmen for the public schools could well adopt the same, and that these latter should especially take care to refrain from such statements as these:

1. That private schools are less democratic and less American than public schools.
2. That individual members of the Catholic Church who attack the public schools are invariably speaking officially for the Church as a whole.
3. That Catholics want to destroy the American public school system.
4. That all the misfortunes of public education are due to the machinations of the Catholic clergy.

Considerable ground-clearing remains before partnership on a national scale can be achieved, but the above suggestions indicate the tools—understanding and tact—which will bring partnership nearer each year.

American society generally approves of the values of religious education. Witness the ferment in the past decade to bring moral and religious programs at least within reach of the public school. Moreover, an awareness is growing that the sheer dimensions of the Catholic school system make its needs and interests more than the concern of the Catholic community. The social realities of today are not the realities of yesteryear. In its own time American society will translate its appreciation of the religious school into a corresponding pattern of appropriate support. To predict this is not to imply any simple or overnight solution to the dual problem of religion in public education and public support for the religious school. As John Courtney Murray has suggested, "The solution, like the creation of the problem itself, will be the work of generations."

It is important that the complexities of the issue be respected. The American people, however, have approached other delicate problems of culture and freedom with honesty, fairness, and sympathy. America's "school problem" one day will be resolved in the same spirit.